T0294526

How to
Close a Museum

How to Close a Museum

A Practical Guide

Susana Smith Bautista

ROWMAN & LITTLEFIELD
Lanham • Boulder • New York • London

Published by Rowman & Littlefield
An imprint of The Rowman & Littlefield Publishing Group, Inc.
4501 Forbes Boulevard, Suite 200, Lanham, Maryland 20706
www.rowman.com

6 Tinworth Street, London SE11 5AL, United Kingdom

British Library Cataloguing in Publication Information Available

Library of Congress Cataloging-in-Publication Data

Names: Bautista, Susana Smith, 1966- author.
Title: How to close a museum : a practical guide / Susana Smith Bautista.
Description: Lanham : Rowman & Littlefield, [2021] | Includes
    bibliographical references and index.
Identifiers: LCCN 2021005868 (print) | LCCN 2021005869 (ebook) | ISBN
    9781538148976 (cloth) | ISBN 9781538148983 (paperback) | ISBN
    9781538148990 (epub)
Subjects: LCSH: Museums—United States—Management. | Museums—Law and
    legislation—United States. | Museum finance—United States.
Classification: LCC AM121 .B38 2021 (print) | LCC AM121 (ebook) | DDC
    069/.068—dc23
LC record available at https://lccn.loc.gov/2021005868
LC ebook record available at https://lccn.loc.gov/2021005869

I dedicate this book to my father, Leonard William Smith, who leaned over to whisper one word to my mother when he met her, taking a test in a German class in 1961. "Courage," he said. Courage was what she needed that morning, and for fifty-eight years they gave each other courage. Whether you are closing a museum, opening a museum, or just struggling within a museum, take courage, and share it with others.

Contents

Preface

This book began after I permanently closed the Pasadena Museum of California Art in October 2018. I knew that I wanted to tell the story of what happened, but it took me a while to get over the very stressful experience. It changed my life, but it also changed so many other lives. After I first went public with my story—at the California Association of Museums conference in March 2020—I was astonished at the overwhelmingly positive response from colleagues and strangers. They wanted to know what happened, why, how, what could have been done differently, and what I learned. Certainly I wasn't the only person that had ever been involved in a museum closure, but I was one of the few that would talk about it in public. That conference took place just at the beginning of COVID-19. Museums started to close temporarily, laying off staff, cutting hours, worrying about their future, and some even announced their permanent closure. It was then that I knew what was needed—a book to guide museums through the difficult experience of closing. More than that, however, I wanted to encourage museums to plan for the possibility of closure just like they plan for so many other things, both positive and negative. Although I was well aware of the problems at the Pasadena Museum of California Art, and was openly working to address them with the Board of Directors, I was absolutely taken by surprise by the board's unilateral decision to close. It is my sincere wish that as museum trustees, leaders, staff, consultants, students, volunteers, and supporters all read this book, they will adopt a different attitude about closure and consider each of their roles and responsibilities. Plan ahead, discuss openly, embrace the unexpected and the unconventional, be responsible, generous, and be courageous above all.

I want to thank Charles Harmon, senior executive acquisitions editor at Rowman & Littlefield, for his commitment to the field of museums, for believing in the need for this book, and for all his support and kindness. My amazing colleagues Natalie Moreno-Cason and Mark Stenroos from the Pasadena Museum of California Art were vital in helping me objectively remember what happened, reminding me that great things can come out of adversities. For the case studies that are presented throughout this book, I was fortunate to speak with current and former staff from many different museums. I am grateful for their candor and reflection, even though it sometimes brought back difficult memories, whether their museums closed permanently or averted disaster. Sean Kelley, from the Eastern State Penitentiary Historic Site in Philadelphia, brought a lighthearted touch to the mistakes and failures that happen in museums. Adam Rozan, from the National Museum of American History, was a valuable collaborator in seeking out and studying museums that closed. John R. Dichtl, from the American Association for State and Local History, was generous with his time and knowledge, helping me to better understand the struggles of small museums, history museums, and historic house museums. Elizabeth Merritt from the Center for the Future of Museums at the American Alliance of Museums was incredibly supportive, sharing her own list of closed museums and taking the time to contribute to the book. Her essential work on scenario planning and strategic foresight is a gift to all museums. Attorney Una Jost was a wealth of information on the legal procedures and resources, and an invaluable partner during the actual dissolution process at the Pasadena Museum of California Art.

Most importantly, I am deeply grateful to my husband Juan Felipe Vallejo, my son Nicolas, and my dog Meli, for their unconditional and unending love and understanding during an unbelievably difficult year. Their admiration for my accomplishments pushes me to do my best. They make me laugh, they wash dishes and fold clothes, they put up with all my emotions, and they take care of me. I thank my mother for giving me a strong work ethic, and I thank my father for giving me courage. I acknowledge and celebrate that it is only with the love and support of family, friends, and professional colleagues that we get through hard times and can find the strength and focus and determination to make a positive difference. Closing a museum is no different. It takes a village, so make sure that you have one, then take care of it.

1

Introduction

The title of this book—*How to Close a Museum*—is really a misnomer, because there is no *single* resource that will serve as a practical guide for *all* museums. We recognize an incredibly diverse museum field—from museums with no collections to living collections to encyclopedic collections, to historic homes and university museums, to private museums and public museums with various governing bodies—with legal requirements for dissolution that vary state by state. Each museum will also find itself in varying situations with regard to its Bylaws, Articles of Incorporation, financial condition, community relations, and any legal restrictions or encumbrances. This book focuses largely on nonprofit museums that have received a tax-exempt status from the Internal Revenue Service, known as their 501(c)(3), in most cases. While there are many museums that successfully operate as for-profit businesses, their process of closure does not involve a dissolution pursuant to—and approved in accordance with—state and federal legal requirements. Nevertheless, there are some for-profit corporations that have museums (which are nonprofit, part of nonprofit corporate foundations, or part of the for-profit organization) that also experience permanent closures.

This book is intended to provide all museum staff, boards, volunteers, donors, and students a better understanding about the complex and mysterious process of dissolution—from legal, ethical, and practical perspectives—in order to direct open conversations surrounding a closure that need to take place, to encourage museums to plan ahead, to recognize early indicators, to imagine scenarios, and to consider several ways to react including closure alternatives. This book also focuses on museums in the United States, as laws are different in other countries. For example, national collections in France are "inalienable" and cannot be sold without an act of Parliament. In the Netherlands, if an object was donated, it must be first offered back to the donor, and if it was acquired with government funds, it must first be offered to another Dutch museum.[1]

The next thing to clear up is that this book is in no way meant to encourage museums to close. The fact that this book was written during the COVID-19 pandemic in 2020–2021 indicates the sad reality that many museums have already closed and will continue to close because of this unexpected external crisis. But actually, there have been, and will always be, natural disasters and unforeseen catastrophes that push some museums over the edge. Many US museums suffered after the 9/11 attacks in New York in 2001, after the Great Recession in 2008, after Hurricane Katrina in New Orleans, and after the wildfires in California, and museums in Europe suffered during World War II. Many more museums decide to permanently close (or are forced to close) for reasons that are more internally focused, such as mission shift and change of focus, loss of founders and major donors, change in governance structure, and certainly financial problems. Miriam Posner, assistant professor of information studies and digital humanities at the University of California, Los Angeles, writes about "Failed Museums" following the Great Recession. Selecting six museums that closed, she offers this reflection,

> These failed museums offer not only cautionary tales and warnings, but valuable illustrations of the nature of collections, the life of artifacts and the infrastructure of cultural institutions. They show us that museums are not handed down from on high. They are fallible, sometimes messy projects that rely on a wide range of stakeholders and networks of support.[2]

This book is intended as a step-by-step guide to dissolution when museums have made that difficult decision—whether the decision comes unexpectedly or through a planning process—and as a guide for all museums that undergo regular planning processes, and in particular those museums that are experiencing difficulties. The American Alliance of Museums (AAM) reports that in 2012,

> Economic difficulties also spurred increased attention to strategic planning . . . with 34% of museums reporting a change in strategic plans (including the creation of a new strategic plan) to reflect changes in economic condition. Museums that experienced moderate to severe economic stress were twice as likely to engage in this kind of strategic planning.[3]

As part of best practices and national (and international) standards for museums that are intended to minimize risk and plan for the future, museums are encouraged to create core documents such as a Collections Management Policy, Disaster Preparedness Plan or Emergency Response Plan, Strategic

Institutional Plan, and even a Succession Plan and Code of Ethics, among other plans and policies. The goal is always to preserve the collections and buildings for future generations, and to ensure the safety of staff and visitors. Yet when all these aforementioned documents address that unforeseen future, there is one glaring omission—what to do when faced with total failure. Every plan is designed to prevent failure, yet the reality is that museums do sometimes fail because of the many reasons we have just cited. We know that many (and probably more) small businesses and for-profit corporations regularly fail for all these same reasons.

If you are reading this book while you are in the very midst of a crisis (internal or external), you may think that all this talk about planning and closure alternatives is simply useless; there is absolutely no time for that and what you need now is swift action. I hear you because I was there. After fourteen months as executive director of the Pasadena Museum of California Art spent trying desperately to save a struggling small art museum with no collection, the chairman of the board suddenly decided to propose to the full board that the museum close permanently, and immediately. He notified me two days before the board meeting, at which all board members agreed to close. The final vote was taken five days later, without having asked staff about the museum's obligations, fundraising, finances, staffing, or programming, and certainly with no plan in hand. As you will read about in greater detail in chapters 4 and 5, this was *not* an ideal way to close a museum. It has been a long process of reflection and evaluation since then, conducted together with former staff and in conversation with the museum field through a panel presentation at the California Association of Museums conference in 2020 (first in-person and then virtually).[4] This book will guide readers on all of the steps to take, when to take them, and how to take care of themselves in the course of what will be an extremely stressful and emotional period.

The parts that are most relevant for these desperate situations are chapter 2 ("Legal Overview"), emergency appeals in chapter 4 ("Planning for Closure"), and all of chapter 5 ("Step-by-Step Closing a Museum"). I cannot stress enough how important ethical considerations are to this process— discussed in chapter 3 under the intentionally cryptic heading "Above and Beyond." Consider this chapter as your intimate advisor and use the talking points when you have those difficult conversations with Boards of Directors, with funders, staff, or as you lay awake at night trying to find answers and not forget anything. The responsibility that all museums have to society, the public, and their cultures and communities (regardless of their governance or structure) should be foremost in their thinking when they plan to operate, just as when they plan to close. The relationships that museums have forged over years of service and partnerships will guide the decisions they make, and *how* they choose to close. Be very clear that you do have a choice. Communities and members can be vital allies during these critical times—supporting and defending museums such as the Detroit Institute of Arts in Michigan or the US Space & Rocket Center in Huntsville, Alabama—or communities can angrily rise up against museums with public protests and lawsuits, sometimes forming incorporated organizations and creating alliances with museum staff. Examples of the latter include the Barnes Foundation in Pennsylvania; Copia: The American Center for Wine, Food & the Arts in Napa Valley, California; the Laguna Art Museum in California; and the Corcoran Gallery of Art in Washington, DC, among many others. In these unfortunate cases, opposition is directed at museum leaders and not at the institution itself, which critics are desperately trying to preserve. This book will help readers to prepare for resistance, both internal and external, and learn from the examples of other museums.

The case studies that are included throughout the book focus on the conditions of closure and not as much on why the museums closed, how the closures could have been prevented, or what went wrong; a separate book for each case would be required because of their complexity. They are meant as a snapshot to convey how different types of museums under various conditions faced different challenges and outcomes. I was fortunate to connect with many museum professionals who were involved with these cases. Some former staff are eager to discuss their experiences and reflect on lessons learned, in the hopes of helping others in the museum field. Other former staff are constrained by nondisclosure agreements that they signed upon departing the museum, and still others have personal reasons for not wanting to discuss the difficult museum closures that they experienced. If you find that one of these cases resonates with your own museum experience, I encourage you to try and contact the individuals involved and dive deeper into researching that particular closure.

It is important to note that not all the case studies ended in permanent closure. Many stories of museums came very, very close, but instead survived for different reasons that are discussed briefly in the case studies, and in greater detail in chapter 4. Planning helps us to imagine several alternate futures and how your museum might react and prepare accordingly. AAM's Center for the Future of Museum's founding director Elizabeth Merritt writes about the importance of forecasting and scenario planning, especially when faced with the worst-case scenario of the highest impact. This type of planning can alert museums to crucial indicators and red flags so that you can identify and potentially minimize risks, thereby avoiding permanent closure. Some of these closure alternatives include mergers and acquisitions, scaling down, and emergency appeals. Yet even the Herculean efforts that museums make to survive do not preclude the need to always consider the possibility of closure and to plan accordingly.

There are many ways to close a museum, as you will read about in the case studies, and not all of them require a legal dissolution process. It is necessary to understand all of these distinctions because, during times of crisis, we often see headlines and official reports about museums closing. While the crises are dangerous indeed, remember that not all museum closures are final, and not all are disastrous. Chapter 4 will discuss the lifecycle of a nonprofit, which can explain how certain museums plan for closure by voluntary dissolution, ensuring that their museum's legacy, collections, and staff are well taken care of for the future. Museums can decide to merge their buildings and collections, sometimes resulting in a completely new organization with a renewed focus. Chapters 3 and 4 will provide tips on how to best plan a merger, what questions need to be asked, and when a merger becomes an acquisition. Regardless of the amount of time you have to plan, these questions will lead your museum to consider its values and priorities; what would you sacrifice first to save the museum, and what needs to remain for your museum to still function and provide a public benefit? Is it your staff, executive salaries and bonuses, unused collections, public programs, or property? You will need to weigh the priorities of your own museum—its history, Bylaws and Articles of Incorporation—with the needs of your community, the standards and guidelines of the professional museum field, and certainly the law.

Read this book when your museum has decided to permanently close, read this book if your museum is going through difficulties or significant changes, read this book if your museum is in the process of strategic or scenario planning, and finally, read this book *before* you even think of starting a new museum. Alexander Graham Bell (1847–1922) was quoted in the *Winona Times* as saying, "When one door closes another door opens; but we often look so long and so regretfully upon the closed door that we do not see the one which has opened for us."[5] We may also know this popular saying as, "Every cloud has a silver lining," or in Spanish as "No hay mal que por bien no venga." Closure is not the end, and not every closure can be considered a failure. Can your museum recover, and if so, will you innovate, improve, and shift your focus? Imagine what that would look like. Disruptions can lead to innovation, improvisation, and growth for organizations, as well as for communities and for individuals. No matter what happens in the end, every museum has a legacy, which can be shaped beforehand with planning, open conversations, and thoughtful decisions as discussed in chapter 3. Be open to the closure planning process, which may offer nontraditional ways to adapt or to give back, and which also may bring last-minute miracles. Museums should close with the same integrity and dedication that they operate. This is the best way to provide public benefit.

NOTES

1. Nina Siegal, "Many Museums Won't Survive the Virus. How Do You Close One Down?" *New York Times*, April 29, 2020, accessed June 10, 2020, https://www .nytimes.com/2020/04/29/arts/design/how-do-you-close-a-museum.html.

2. The six museums are the Higgins Armory Museum, the National Museum of Crime and Punishment, the Women's Museum, Liberace Museum, Paul H. Jensen Arctic Museum, and Fresno Metropolitan Museum of Art. Miriam Posner, "Failed Museums," accessed July 19, 2020, http://miriamposner.com/omeka/exhibits/show/ fail/intro.

3. American Alliance of Museums, "America's Museums Reflect Slow Economic Recovery in 2012," accessed September 25, 2020, https://www.aam-us.org/wp -content/uploads/2018/01/acme-2013-final.pdf.

4. Susana Bautista, Elena Brokaw, and Jeannette Kihs, "Museums on the Edge: Stories of Transformation and Failure," online presentation at the California Association of Museums Lunch & Learn, March 6, 2020, https://www.youtube.com/ watch?v=WhWF59i3rrA&t=3s.

5. "Alexander Graham Bell Quotes," Your Dictionary, accessed November 23, 2020, https://quotes.yourdictionary.com/author/alexander-graham-bell/.

2

Legal Overview
Dissolution of a 501(c)(3) Public Benefit Corporation

DISSOLUTION GOVERNED BY STATE LAW

According to the National Council of Nonprofits, *"Dissolution is a change in your nonprofit's corporate status that is governed by state law."* The most important part of the closure process of any museum is understanding the laws that govern nonprofit organizations, and how those laws govern any changes to the museum as a corporate entity. Both state and federal governmental bodies are involved in administering these laws. These include, at the state level, the Attorney General, Secretary of State, and Franchise Tax Board, and at the federal level, the Internal Revenue Service. This chapter provides a summary review of legal options and requirements for dissolution, which may vary from state to state.[1] Examples given here will refer to laws of specific states, but readers must verify applicable laws in their own states. Various factors need to be considered in assessing the appropriate path to dissolution, including a museum's entity status, entity type, activities, debts, and length of operation.

It must also be mentioned here that this information, and resources included at the end, are for general information purposes only and do not constitute legal advice. They are in no way meant to suggest that museums undertake this process on their own. Dissolution is a complex process, different for every museum, and more complex the larger the organization with more staff and assets. It is highly recommended for museums to engage a lawyer specializing in nonprofit organization law. Nonprofit attorney Una Jost explains, "Nonprofit clients are often surprised to learn how complex, or how lengthy, the dissolution process can be. Depending on the circumstances that give rise to the need to consider dissolution, the museum may also be confronted

with addressing both external and internal challenges in terms of staff morale, economic downturns impacting revenue stream, publicity crises, etc."[2]
Often museums may need to work with additional counsel, including those
that specialize in human resources or employment law, trusts and estates, and
contracts. Even if the museum has an attorney on the Board of Directors, it is
advisable to seek an outside attorney or law firm for this process to avoid any
perception of conflict of interest.

THE INTERNAL REVENUE SERVICE

Perhaps the most important legal benefit (and often constraint) for museums
is their federal tax-exempt status, which is conferred upon them by the Internal Revenue Service (IRS). There are twenty-nine different types of nonprofit
organizations ranging from cemetery companies to black lung benefit trusts,
each listed under a different subsection of the 501(c) section of the Internal
Revenue Code.[3] Most museums are established as 501(c)(3) organizations,
which the Code defines as:

> An organization must be organized and operated exclusively for exempt pur-
> poses set forth in section 501(c)(3), and none of its earnings may inure to any
> private shareholder or individual. In addition, it may not be an action organi-
> zation, i.e., it may not attempt to influence legislation as a substantial part of
> its activities and it may not participate in any campaign activity for or against
> political candidates.[4]

The IRS lists the following *exclusive* purposes for which an organization
may qualify for exemption from federal income tax: religious, charitable,
scientific, testing for public safety, literacy, educational, fostering national
or international amateur sports competition, and the prevention of cruelty to
children or animals.[5] Museums are specifically listed under the category of
educational organizations, along with zoos and planetariums. The IRS defines
the term education as: "the instruction or training of individuals for the purpose of improving or developing their capabilities, or the instruction of the
public on subjects useful to individuals and beneficial to the community."[6]

The Code further states that such organizations are "commonly referred to
as charitable organizations" that are "eligible to receive tax-deductible contributions in accordance with Code section 170." Don Fullerton, an economist
and professor at the University of Illinois, describes this as "an extra incentive
to make charitable donations through the deduction against income tax or
estate tax for such gifts. At the current top marginal, personal income-tax rate
of 28 percent, a dollar gift only costs the taxpayer 72 cents, because the gov-

ernment gives up 28 cents that might otherwise be collected."[7] In discussing the justification for public support (or what Fullerton calls "implicit subsidy" and "indirect federal aid"), he states that the "total value to the users of the service at least equals the total cost of providing the service." The notion of *benefits* is important here, as benefits flow to the general public and not just to those who visit the museum, and museums are "nonrival" in that many people can benefit without using it up—hence, the determination that museums are public benefit corporations.[8]

The Internal Revenue Code regulates how each nonprofit organization must be established as a legal entity (a corporation, trust, or association), with written articles of organization that may be a corporate charter (with articles of incorporation), a trust instrument, articles of association, or "any other written instrument by which the organization was created." These documents must include certain provisions such as a purpose clause and a dissolution clause. The IRS suggests the following language for the dissolution clause:

> Upon the dissolution of the corporation, assets shall be distributed for one or more exempt purposes within the meaning of section 501(c)(3) of the Internal Revenue Code, or the corresponding section of any future federal tax code, or shall be distributed to the federal government, or to a state or local government, for a public purpose. Any such assets not so disposed of shall be disposed of by a Court of Competent Jurisdiction of the county in which the principal office of the corporation is then located, exclusively for such purposes or to such organization or organizations, as said Court shall determine, which are organized and operated exclusively for such purposes.[9]

The IRS monitors the operation of nonprofit museums to ensure public access and educational activities, and likewise it also regulates their dissolution and disposal of assets, which will be discussed further in this chapter.

TYPES OF MUSEUM CLOSURES

As the introduction noted, there is a difference between temporary and permanent museum closures. Dissolution refers to *permanent* closure. In addition, dissolution can be either voluntary or involuntary. Even if a museum is intended to be temporarily closed, it must justify that it continues to provide educational or charitable activities in accordance with its Articles of Incorporation and Bylaws, since inactivity for more than a year is grounds for *involuntary* or *compulsory dissolution*. Remember that voluntary dissolution is only a legal term that indicates that the closure has been decided by the museum's Board of Directors of its own volition, however difficult and undesirable that decision may be. Let's first talk about involuntary dissolution, which is less known and occurs less frequently.

Grounds for Involuntary Dissolution

In California, Corporations Code CORP §6510 sets forth the following grounds for involuntary dissolution:

1. The corporation has abandoned its activity for more than one year.
2. The corporation has an even number of directors who are equally divided and cannot agree as to the management of its affairs, so that its activities can no longer be conducted to advantage or so that there is danger that its property will be impaired or lost or its activities impaired and the members are so divided into factions that they cannot elect a board consisting of an uneven number.
3. There is internal dissension and two or more factions of members in the corporation are so deadlocked that its activities can no longer be conducted with advantage.
4. When during any four-year period or when all voting power has been exercised at two consecutive meetings or in two written ballots for the election of directors, whichever period is shorter, the members have failed to elect successors to directors whose terms have expired or would have expired upon election of their successors.
5. Those in control of the corporation have been guilty of or have knowingly countenanced persistent and pervasive fraud, mismanagement or abuse of authority or the corporation's property is being misapplied or wasted by its directors or officers.
6. Liquidation is reasonably necessary as the corporation is failing and has continuously failed to carry out its purposes.
7. The period for which the corporation was formed has terminated without extension of such period.
8. The corporation is required to dissolve under the terms of any article provision adopted pursuant to subdivision (a), paragraph (2), clause (i), of Section 5132.[10]

In addition, involuntary dissolution may be initiated by the state Attorney General based on the following grounds:

1. The corporation has seriously offended against any provision of the statutes regulating corporations or charitable organizations.

2. The corporation has fraudulently abused or usurped corporate privileges or powers.
3. The corporation has violated any provision of law by any act or default which under the law is a ground for forfeiture of corporate existence.
4. The corporation has failed to pay to the Franchise Tax Board for a period of five years any tax imposed upon it by the Bank and Corporation Tax Law.

Actions for involuntary dissolution can be filed by either the state Attorney General, or the directors, members, or other authorized persons of the museum.

Grounds for Administrative Dissolution

Administrative dissolution is also considered involuntary and may occur if a museum fails to file its state tax return or pay certain tax liabilities. For the former reason, the museum may be *suspended* by the Franchise Tax Board (FTB). While a museum is suspended, it cannot conduct business within that state, enforce legal contracts, or initiate legal action to defend itself in lawsuits, and it loses all rights to use its name. If the museum has been suspended for at least two years, the FTB has grounds to institute an administrative dissolution of the museum. The FTB will proceed by mailing to the museum notification of the pending administrative dissolution. In addition, the Secretary of State will list the name and file number of the museum on its website for sixty days, along with information about how the museum may object to the administrative dissolution. If no response is received within the 60-day period, or if the museum is unsuccessful in curing its suspension status, the museum will be administratively dissolved. With an administrative dissolution, any liabilities for taxes, interest, and penalties are abated, and there will be no further action taken by the FTB to collect these amounts. In addition, if a museum fails to file its annual federal information return for three years in a row, the IRS will automatically revoke its tax-exempt status and publish the museum's revocation status. There is no appeals process with the IRS for the automatic revocation, and the museum must apply for reinstatement in order to be restored to its exempt status.

Public Counsel (the largest pro bono public interest law firm) offers an interesting suggestion for nonprofit organizations that are out of compliance with the Franchise Tax Board and have decided to pursue a dissolution. If the organization has no assets or outstanding liabilities, then Public Counsel (2017) proposes that "it may be easier to simply wait for administrative dissolution, rather than to file the dissolution paperwork. A nonprofit wanting to dissolve should therefore not respond to the FTB notice of a pending admin-istrative dissolution."[11] This option also has the added benefit that all accrued taxes are abated. When this occurs, the California nonprofit will have consid-ered its ability to conduct business in California as *administratively surren-dered*. However, note that administrative dissolution should be intentionally pursued *only* if the museum has no assets, is not engaged in operations, and has no intention to continue to operate.

Caution: Outstanding debts and liabilities survive involuntary dissolution. California law requires museums to "adequately provide for" any debts by of-fering payment to creditors. If a museum has outstanding debts and liabilities, an involuntary dissolution will not wipe away those responsibilities; involun-tary dissolution does not change any liabilities of the museum, or any liabili-ties of directors, nor does it change the ability of the state Attorney General to enforce those liabilities. In seeking to adequately provide for any debts, if the claimant cannot be located or if the debt is subject to dispute or contingency, the museum board can work with the state Attorney General to develop a repayment plan, liquidation, or bankruptcy. A museum cannot be forced into *bankruptcy*, but the board can vote to declare bankruptcy. Bankruptcy can be a very expensive process, supervised by a federal bankruptcy court, and does not automatically result in dissolution. *Liquidation* is included in the above-mentioned California Corporations Code (#6) as one of the grounds for involuntary dissolution. Any distribution or dispersal of assets to creditors or other parties must conform to the museum's Articles of Incorporation and Bylaws, and not be restricted or encumbered by donors.

The museum board may also request a *court-supervised dissolution* (still considered involuntary), which would protect the board from liability be-cause it avoids any improper board distribution of assets. In this option, the court may appoint a *receiver* who would be empowered to conduct the wind-ing up process for a fee (paid by the nonprofit) under the court's ultimate supervision. A museum board can also arrange for a federal agency or another "financially responsible person" to assume payment or guarantee the debt, but it must first conduct an analysis of the financial capacity of this agency or person. Another option is for the museum board to deposit an adequate amount (what they believe to be "in good faith") of cash, stocks, or property with the State Controller, a bank, or trust company, for creditors to later submit claims. More about the ethical dispersal of assets will be discussed in the next chapter, regarding original donor intentions, museum legacy, and adherence to museum mission and values.

Voluntary Dissolution

We have just discussed two processes for involuntary dissolution (administrative and court-supervised or judicial). *Voluntary dissolution* has three distinct processes: standard, short form, and voluntary with pre-dissolution tax abatement. Of these, the most common is the standard (or long form) process, which will be discussed in greater detail in this chapter, as this process applies to the majority of nonprofit US museums. *Short form* is a streamlined process intended for nonprofit corporations that were created in error, have not issued memberships, and have been in existence for less than two years. The California short form requires nonprofits to have no debts or liabilities (other than tax liabilities that have been paid or assumed), to have filed a final tax return with the Franchise Tax Board, to have distributed any remaining assets to the "persons entitled thereto," and to have a majority of directors or incorporators authorize the dissolution. Louisiana law stipulates that for the short form, a museum must have no debt and no *immovable* property (most commonly real estate) at the time of dissolution. If a nonprofit has debt or immovable property, then the *long form* voluntary dissolution applies. California also allows for a *pre-dissolution tax abatement* authorizing the Franchise Tax Board to abate any unpaid qualified taxes, interest, and penalties assessed for the taxable years a nonprofit certifies that it was not doing business in the state.

Ohio Nonprofit Corporation Law sets forth its procedures for *voluntary dissolution*, under Chapter 1702.47.[12]

(A) A corporation may be dissolved voluntarily in the manner provided in this section.
(B) A resolution of dissolution for a corporation shall set forth:
  (1) That the corporation elects to be dissolved;
  (2) Any additional provision deemed necessary with respect to the proposed dissolution and winding up.
(C) The directors may adopt a resolution of dissolution in the following cases:
  (1) When the corporation has been adjudged bankrupt or has made a general assignment for the benefit of creditors;
  (2) By leave of the court, when a receiver has been appointed in a general creditors' suit or in any suit in which the affairs of the corporation are to be wound up;
  (3) When substantially all of the assets have been sold at judicial sale or otherwise;
  (4) When the period of existence of the corporation specified in its articles has expired.
(D)
  (1) The voting members at a meeting held for that purpose may adopt a resolution of dissolution by the affirmative vote of a majority of the

voting members present in person or, if permitted, by mail, by proxy, or by the use of authorized communications equipment, if a quorum is present or, if the articles or the regulations provide or permit, by the affirmative vote of a greater or lesser proportion or number of the voting members, and by the affirmative vote of the voting members or the affirmative vote of the voting members of any particular class that is required by the articles or the regulations. Notice of the meeting of the members shall be sent to all the members who would be entitled to vote at the meeting by mail, overnight delivery service, or any authorized communications equipment.

(2) For purposes of division (D)(1) of this section, participation by a voting member at a meeting through the use of any of the means of communication described in that division constitutes presence in person of that voting member at the meeting for purposes of determining a quorum.

(E) Upon the adoption of a resolution of dissolution, a certificate shall be prepared, on a form prescribed by the secretary of state, setting forth the following:

(1) The name of the corporation;

(2) A statement that a resolution of dissolution has been adopted;

(3) A statement of the manner of adoption of that resolution, and, in the case of its adoption by the directors, a statement of the basis for the adoption;

(4) The place in this state where its principal office is or is to be located;

(5) The names and addresses of its directors and officers;

(6) The name and address of its statutory agent;

(7) The date of dissolution, if other than the filing date.

(F) The certificate described in division (E) of this section shall be signed by any authorized officer, unless the officer fails to execute and file the certificate within thirty days after the adoption of the resolution, or upon any date specified in the resolution as the date upon which the certificate is to be filed, or upon the expiration of any period specified in the resolution as the period within which the certificate is to be filed, whichever is latest, in which event the certificate of dissolution may be signed by any three voting members and shall set forth a statement that the persons signing the certificate are voting members and are filing the certificate because of the failure of the officers to do so.

(G) A certificate of dissolution, filed with the secretary of state, shall be accompanied by:

(1) A receipt, certificate, or other evidence from the director of job and family services showing that all contributions due from the corporation as an employer have been paid, that such payment has been adequately guaranteed, or that the corporation is not subject to such contributions;

(2) A receipt, certificate, or other evidence showing that the corporation has paid all taxes imposed under the laws of this state that are or will be due from the corporation on the date of the dissolution, or that such payment has been adequately guaranteed;

(3) In lieu of the receipt, certificate, or other evidence described in division (G)(1) or (2) of this section, an affidavit of one or more of the persons executing the certificate of dissolution or of an officer of the corporation containing a statement of the date upon which the particular department, agency, or authority was advised in writing of the scheduled effective date of the dissolution and was advised in writing of the acknowledgement by the corporation of the applicability of section 1702.55 of the Revised Code.

(H) Upon the filing of a certificate of dissolution and those accompanying documents or on a later date specified in the certificate that is not more than ninety days after the filing, the corporation shall be dissolved.

In comparison, the State of Massachusetts sets forth the following procedures for voluntary dissolution in Section 11A: Dissolution; voluntary; charitable corporation:

(a) A charitable corporation constituting a public charity organized under any general or special law, which desires to voluntarily wind up and close its affairs, may authorize its dissolution in accordance with this section. This section shall constitute the sole method for the voluntary dissolution of a charitable corporation.

(b) A petition for dissolution shall be authorized by vote of a majority of the corporation's Board of Directors entitled to vote thereon; provided, however, that if the corporation has 1 or more classes of members, the corporation may, in its articles of incorporation, in a by-law adopted by the incorporators under section 3 or in a by-law adopted by the members, assign the power of authorization to the members acting by majority vote of the members entitled to vote thereon or provide that the exercise of the power shall be subject to approval by the members.

(c) If the corporation has no remaining assets, the petition for dissolution shall be submitted to the division of public charities of the office of the attorney general setting forth in substance the grounds of the application for dissolution together with the forms, affidavits and information as the division from time to time may prescribe. If the division is satisfied that the corporation has or will become inactive and that its dissolution would be in the public interest, the division may approve the dissolution of the corporation.

(d) If the corporation has remaining assets, the petition for its dissolution shall be filed in the supreme judicial court setting forth in substance the grounds for the application for dissolution and requesting the court to authorize the administration of its funds for similar public charitable purposes as the court may determine. The supreme judicial court may, by rule or order, provide that the petition and court authorization are not required for dissolutions approved by the division upon receipt of the forms, affidavits and information as the division may require if the corporation has net assets no greater than such amount as the court may provide in the rule or order or in such other situations as the court may provide.[13]

CASE IN POINT:

Copia: The American Center for Wine, Food & the Arts, Napa, California

Founded by successful vintners Robert and Margaret Modavi with an initial gift of $20 million (plus what they paid for the land in 1996), Copia opened in 2001 with a 240,000-square-foot facility (plus 3 1/2 acres of gardens) in downtown Napa. It was a hybrid invention connecting agriculture, viticulture, and material culture. It included a rare books library, 74-seat demonstration kitchen called The Food Forum, wine tasting table, gourmet restaurant, café, gift shop, art gallery, 260-seat theater, 10,000-square-foot outdoor concert area, an outdoor Children's Garden and Kitchen, and a large parking lot. Many locals considered it an impetus for economic development that brought tourists to the area while also serving the local community. Attendance was projected to be 300,000 annually. This wasn't so easy though, as tourists don't often go into downtown but prefer to stay on the highway roads between the vineyards. Also, the local community was not accustomed to philanthropy and art, and major vintners in the valley preferred to support their local communities. Operational expenses were huge from the onset, but the largest expense was a municipal bond of $77.6 million from 1999 to cover "construction and equipping of the center's new facilities." Even after refinancing in 2007, then later selling five acres of the property, the museum continued to lose money each year with substantially fewer visitors than anticipated. They had to raise $2.5 million a year just to pay the bond, then the terms changed and it became $6 million a year. Earned income was very strong and comprised 70 percent of the budget, but then roads were closed due to flood control. Before Robert Mondavi died in 2008, he made substantial gifts to the Oxbow School of art and academics in Napa and the University of California, Davis, whose dean served on Copia's board. Some say that this money should have gone to Copia to establish an endowment, which might have saved the museum. After founding director Peggy Loar left in early 2005, a second director came from the San Francisco Ballet for only six months. Garry McGuire moved from the boardroom and became CEO in 2007. Staff was cut almost 40 percent, admission was cut from $12.50 to $5 a person, and the museum focused just on wine. Nevertheless, it continued to lose money, made worse by the recession. Copia had a bond-financed debt of more than $79 million, and assets of around $30 million (including a $7.3 million reserve fund). There was talk of selling the property, leasing part of it and moving to San Francisco, but nothing materialized. Copia leaders were unrealistically optimistic at wanting to keep operating during the reorganization. They pronounced, "The decision to restructure the business through a Chapter 11 filing should provide us with the opportunity to strengthen our balance sheet, create a more efficient expense structure and ultimately position our public-benefit corporation to compete more effectively."[1] McGuire also spoke about "an expansion to a San Francisco campus, a focus on Web-based operations and the creation of 'the world's largest tasting room.'"[2] The museum's bankruptcy trustee objected to the $2 million line of credit, the judge refused the museum's request, and McGuire resigned. Copia filed for bankruptcy protection at the end of 2008. In 2009, a group of local investors, developers, and businessmen formed the Coalition to Preserve Copia, and offered $30 million to ACA Financial Guaranty Corporation in New York (owners of the property and the bond insurers), but their offer was declined. That same year there was a class action lawsuit (*Copia Claims LLC*) against the museum. The judge approved a liquidation plan and creditors agreed to a carve-out settlement, receiving a fraction of their claims. The property was foreclosed by the deed holders and the bond insurer, with all the funds going into a liquidating trust administered by a San Francisco legal firm. The cookbook library was donated to Napa Valley College, the greenhouse and exhibitions moved to Connolly Ranch, a teaching farm nearby, and in 2016 the Culinary Art Institute moved into the buildings. Reflecting on all of Copia's problems, Peggy Loar sadly admitted, "it was a perfect storm."[3]

NOTES

1. Sasha Paulsen, "Copia Files for Bankruptcy," *Napa Valley Register*, December 3, 2008, accessed August 8, 2020, https://napavalleyregister.com/news/local/copia-files-for-bankruptcy/article_7da03b25-e1b4-5ee1-acca-f9d5a7204f93.html.
2. Ibid.
3. Peggy Loar (former founding director/president of Copia), in discussion with the author, August 20, 2020.

CONDUCTING DUE DILIGENCE

Before deciding on which form of dissolution is best for your museum—if it indeed is your museum's final decision to dissolve—FIRST ascertain whether the museum is in good standing with your Secretary of State; SECOND take the time to review some important documents: your museum's Articles of Incorporation, Bylaws, and financial statements (Statement of Cash Flows, Statement of Activities, and the Balance Sheet or Statement of Financial Position); and THIRD find a good attorney familiar with nonprofit organization law.

The Secretary of State will not file any dissolution paperwork unless the museum is considered "in good standing," which is why museums should first confirm their status with the Secretary of State. This information can be easily found online with the Secretary of State (for the state of California: https://businesssearch.sos.ca.gov/CBS). If the status is listed as *Active*, then the museum is in good standing. If it is listed as *Suspended*, then the museum should immediately contact the Secretary of State's office to ascertain the cause for suspension and steps needed to cure the suspension. The museum is considered *Revived* when the government agencies that issued the suspension agree the museum is in compliance, with any outstanding governmental fees paid in full. The Secretary of State's office will then issue a *Certificate of Revivor* (or a Certificate of Revival in Nevada, or a Certificate of Renewal and Revival issued by the Delaware Division of Corporations). In New York, before museums can file their Certificate of Dissolution, they must request consent from the New York Department of Taxation and Finance within the state Corporation Tax Dissolution Unit.

The museum's Articles of Incorporation and Bylaws are the core documents that will guide a museum's dissolution process, just as they have guided the museum's incorporation and operations. The Internal Revenue Service requires nonprofit exempt organizations to include a dissolution clause in their Articles of Incorporation, and many states also require such a clause in the Bylaws; sample suggested language for such a dissolution clause is noted earlier in this chapter.

Some museums may have already decided beforehand how to distribute their assets upon dissolution and will have included this information in the dissolution clause of their Bylaws. The Bylaws will also guide the voting process for dissolution—whether a nonprofit has a voting membership that must vote in favor of the dissolution, and whether there must be an affirmative vote in favor of the dissolution by the Board of Directors with a majority of directors in office or by a majority present at the board meeting where there is a quorum.

Financial statements will also reveal any restrictions you should be aware of early on, and which should be part of your board discussions when contemplating dissolution, such as promised and lifetime gifts, donor restricted funds, and bequests. Knowing your museum's current assets and liabilities and cash flow are important in order to determine details about your museum's dissolution, such as the final date of operations, staffing, and creation of a closure budget. Would you need to settle any debts first? Would you need to transfer funds or liquidate any assets to finance the closure process? A longer closure period will generally be more expensive, even if operational expenses are reduced, but it may be necessary to resolve outstanding issues with creditors, donors, and organizational partners regarding exhibitions and public programming. Discuss all these matters both with transparency and in confidentiality with the full board and with senior leadership at the museum, together with the attorney that you have just hired, and create a dissolution plan with as much detail as possible. A formal *Plan of Dissolution* may be required by some states and will incorporate critical information necessary for any dissolution process, such as determining how the assets will be distributed.

Step One: Adopt Board and/or Member Dissolution Resolutions Electing to Wind Up and Dissolve as Appropriate

Ideally, your museum would have thought through its plan of dissolution and is now ready to take the first step in commencing the dissolution process. If you have decided on a *standard* voluntary dissolution, the decision must be approved by the museum board, adopting resolutions electing to wind up and dissolve. It is important that the board dissolution resolutions be properly recorded in the museum's board minutes (or board unanimous written consent), noting if any directors voted by mail, email, telephone, or proxy (if allowed by the Bylaws); the specific vote for each director; and the date. A museum having statutory voting members would also need to adopt resolutions electing to wind up and dissolve the museum. A *Certificate of Election to Wind Up and Dissolve* may also be required if there was *not* 100 percent participation in the vote for dissolution, which is then filed with the Secretary of State or your state's own division, commission, or department. After board dissolution resolutions are approved, the museum must terminate all activities other than those necessary to wind up and dissolve the museum. While most exhibitions, programs, marketing, and fundraising efforts may have stopped long ago, California does allow the board to continue activities that preserve the "goodwill or going concern value" of the museum.

Step Two: File Request with Attorney General for a Written Waiver of
Objections to Any Proposed Distribution of Assets

Next the board should request from the state Attorney General a written
Waiver of Objections to any proposed distribution of assets at least twenty
days prior to the desired distribution date of assets. The transfer of assets must
be consistent with the stated purpose of the museum as set forth in its Articles
of Incorporation, and which is always subject to objections by the state Attorney General. Illinois law states that,

> Under the Charitable Trust Act, a not for profit corporation is considered a
> trustee of a charitable trust if it holds property for any charitable purpose.
> Therefore, funds which are appropriated for the benefit of society at large are
> considered held in charitable trust and the Illinois Attorney General holds vested
> common law power and authority to safeguard these charitable assets.[14]

In California, to request a waiver, a board member or attorney for the museum must send:

1. A letter describing and stating the material facts of the proposed distribution of remaining assets, including which individuals or organizations will receive which assets;
2. A copy of the board's dissolution resolution authorizing the proposed
   distribution of assets;
3. A copy of the museum's current financial statement as of a date within
   90 days of the date of submission of the waiver;
4. A copy of the museum's endorsed-filed copy of the museum's Articles
   of Incorporation and Bylaws, including any amendments, if not already
   on file with the Registrar of Charitable Trusts
5. A copy of the articles of incorporation of any other corporation that is a
   party to the proposed transaction.[15]

In Massachusetts, it is the Supreme Judicial Court that authorizes the transfer
of assets through an *Interlocutory Order*. Upon transfer of assets in con-
formance with the Order, the museum must submit an *Affidavit of Compli-*
ance and an *Affidavit of Receipt* as confirmation.[16] Most states require the
museum's Board of Directors to remain intact until they receive the waiver
letter from the state Attorney General. Because this could take a long time
to process, it may be unfeasible for staff to continue working or for the full
board to continue meeting regularly. Therefore, the board may wish to consider amending the museum Bylaws beforehand if necessary, to allow for a
decreased board size of three to five board members.

Step Three: Wind Up Operations, Pay or Adequately Provide for Payment of Liabilities, and Distribute Assets

In winding up operations, the assets of the museum can be *sold* for fair value, with the proceeds distributed to another museum or another public benefit corporation (subject to its Articles of Incorporation), or assets may be *donated* directly to another museum or other public benefit corporation (again subject to its Articles of Incorporation). The Articles of Incorporation can be amended beforehand to designate new recipients of the corporation's assets if desired, subject to the powers of the Attorney General. However, only after the museum has either paid or adequately provided for payment of liabilities as applicable, and received from the state Attorney General a written waiver of objections to the proposed distribution of assets, should the board proceed with distributing the museum's remaining assets in accordance with its dissolution plan. In certain circumstances, it may take up to a year or more to receive this waiver letter from the state Attorney General, at which point the museum may have already ceased its operations, terminated all staff, and reduced its board to a bare minimum. To address this time lag, once the museum has identified the nonprofit organizations to receive its assets and listed those organizations and corresponding assets in its Plan of Distribution and letter to the state Attorney General requesting a waiver of objections to the proposed distribution of assets, the museum may consider a *provisional* transfer while staff are still employed. If museums pursue this alternative, it is advisable for there to be a written agreement itemizing all the assets, signed by both parties, and including a clause stating that transfer of ownership is subject to the museum receiving its written waiver of objections to the proposed distribution of assets from the state Attorney General.[17]

Step Four: Send Notice of Dissolution and Winding Up to Creditors as Necessary

In meeting the museum's obligation to pay or adequately provide for payment of the museum's liability, it is beneficial for the museum to take advantage of the method for disposing of known claims in the winding up process. To do so, the museum must provide a formal notice of dissolution and winding up to creditors as necessary. In California, the notice must include a mailing address where claims can be sent, the deadline for any submission of claims (at least four months from the date of the written notice), a statement that claims submitted after the deadline will not be accepted, and any information that claimants must include in their submission. If the museum does not hear back from the creditor within the given response period, the creditor will be barred from later making claim to the museum for payment.

*Step Five: File a Certificate of Dissolution with the Secretary of State (or
Articles of Dissolution with Appropriate State Agency)*

Finally, after the winding up and voluntary dissolution is completed, the
museum must file a *Certificate of Dissolution* with the Secretary of State,
along with the state Attorney General's waiver letter. It is important to request that the Secretary of State return a certified copy of the Certificate of
Dissolution to the museum. In California, you must file the Certificate of
Dissolution with the Secretary of State. Florida, however, requires Articles
of Dissolution to be filed with its Department of State's Division of Corporations. Florida sets forth the following voting procedures for filing the Articles
of Dissolution:

- if your nonprofit has members entitled to vote on dissolution, either (a)
  the date of the member meeting at which the resolution to dissolve was
  adopted and a statement that the votes cast was sufficient for approval,
  or (b) a statement that such a resolution was adopted by written consent
  and executed in accordance with section 617.0701 of the Florida Not For
  Profit Corporation Act; and
- if your nonprofit does not have members entitled to vote on dissolution,
  a statement of that fact, the date the resolution to dissolve was adopted
  by the Board of Directors, the number of directors then in office, and the
  number of votes for and against the resolution.[18]

Louisiana requires all incorporators (not members) to approve the dissolution but does not clearly indicate that a board without members can authorize
dissolution. The Articles of Dissolution must also include information about
how the nonprofit's remaining assets will be distributed after all creditors
have been paid. Regarding the distribution of assets, Massachusetts law provides the following:

> Please note that the entity to which the assets are transferred must have a
> charitable purpose similar to that of the dissolving organization or must agree
> to use the assets in accordance with the dissolving organization's purpose. The
> officer's certificate should specify the receiving entity or entities and articulate
> whether the assets and/or property are to be used for the organization's general
> purpose or are restricted to ensure that the assets and property are used in con-
> formance with the dissolving organization's original mission.[19]

Upon receipt of the Articles of Dissolution, the government agency will issue
a public notice.

Step Six: Notify Registrar of Charitable Trusts and File Final IRS Informational Return

All that is left is to notify the Registrar of Charitable Trusts and the Internal Revenue Service. The board must send a certified copy of the Certificate of Dissolution to the Registrar of Charitable Trusts at the state Attorney General's office, together with a final financial report showing a zero balance and no assets. The IRS is informed by the museum filing its final Form 990, which is due by the fifteenth day of the fifth month after final dissolution, along with copies of the board dissolution resolution and affidavit of dissolution. If a museum terminates its operations in the middle of its fiscal year it can still file its Form 990 (or 990-EZ), whenever the dissolution process is completed. The final tax returns should show no remaining liabilities or assets. The IRS also requires the museum to file a Schedule N (Liquidation, Termination, Dissolution, or Significant Disposition of Assets) to the Form 990 (or 990-EZ), which includes the following:

• Description of the assets and any transaction fees associated with the assets' disposal
• Dates of the distribution of each asset
• Assets' fair market value
• Information about the tax-exempt recipients of the assets

Unless exempt, your museum must also file a final state tax return. If your museum has dealings with other state agencies, they should also be notified. These agencies might include the Department of Labor, state licensing authorities such as the Department of Health and Human Services, or the Transportation Agency, Department of Parks and Recreation, Native American Heritage Commission, Department of Education, or Arts Council.

CASE IN POINT:

Corcoran Gallery of Art, Washington, DC

The Corcoran Gallery of Art was first founded in 1869 by William Wilson Corcoran as one of the first fine art galleries in the United States, supported by an endowment "for the perpetual establishment and encouragement of the Fine Arts." It expanded in 1880 to include the Corcoran School of the Arts and Design, which provided an important source of revenue to the gallery with tuition. In 1989, the Corcoran famously canceled a controversial exhibition of Robert Mapplethorpe photographs, in response to condemnation by conservative politicians who did not believe that the federal National Endowment for the Arts should be funding such "morally reprehensible trash." The DC art community protested this act of censorship, and some say the museum was never able to rebuild a close relationship with its local arts and funding community. Corcoran trustee Dr. Armand Hammer underwrote free admission from 1979, but that had ended around this time, and they started to again charge admission. The museum struggled financially for many years, in the shadow of much larger and popular museums in DC with free admission. There was too much deferred maintenance on its large, historic building, and in the early 2000s, they had to abandon plans to build a new wing designed by architect Frank Gehry. The Corcoran sold off property in 2010 for $6.5 million, it sold a seventeenth-century rug at auction in 2013 for $33.8 million, it signed a 99-year lease for its parking lot for $20.5 million, and it still had deficits almost every year. Having exhausted all other ideas, as well as an offer to help from Carnegie Mellon University, the Corcoran Board of Trustees announced in 2012 that they would move the museum to Alexandria, Virginia, and sell the building in DC. By that time, they had essentially stopped all fundraising, grant writing, and even turned down donations. The group "Save the Corcoran" was formed to keep the Corcoran in DC and the collection intact. "The Corcoran name, and the District of Columbia, deserve better," said Jayme McLellan, a member of Save the Corcoran and adjunct faculty at the Corcoran.[1] With the support of pro bono attorneys in DC, the group went to the Attorney General to claim malfeasance. The founder's 1869 trust (which included Corcoran's art collection, some funds, and the Renwick building) and charter, stipulated that the gallery had to remain in DC. The Corcoran was in talks with George Washington University and the University of Maryland to explore other options. The Corcoran petitioned the courts for a cy-près ruling that would modify any restrictions to permit a reorganization, which its lawyers argued "is the next best way to fulfill the original vision."[2] Despite the intervention of the group, in 2014 the Corcoran dissolved and transferred the College of Art and Design and the building to George Washington University, using proceeds from the sale of the rug to restore the building. Corcoran trustees established a new 501(c) (3) called the Corcoran and created a website to provide the public with information (www.Corcoran.org). According to the website, the Corcoran distributed over 19,456 works from its collection to museums and institutions mostly in Washington, DC (the National Gallery of Art had first choice of works), and the museum archives were sent to the Gelman Library at George Washington University.

NOTES

1. "Lawyers for Save the Corcoran Coalition File Formal Complaint, Seek to Intervene in Proceedings to Break the Corcoran Gallery of Art's Historic Deed. Organization Requests for Board to Provide Full Financial Accounting," Save the Corcoran (blog), July 2, 2014, http://savethecorcoran.org/2014/07/02/lawyers -for-save-the-corcoran-coalition-file-formal-complaint-seek-to-intervene -in-proceedings-to-break-the-corcoran-gallery-of-arts-historic-deed-organization -requests-for-board-to-provide/#.X2bl-otlCUm.
2. David Montgomery, "Corcoran Maneuvers to Keep its Art from Leaving the Area," *Washington Post*, June 26, 2014, https://www.washingtonpost.com/ lifestyle/style/corcoran-maneuvers-to-keep-its-art-from-leaving-the-area/ 2014/06/26/0158b1d2-fd3a-11e3-8176-f2c941cf35f1_story.html.

DISTRIBUTION, DISPOSAL, AND DEACCESSION

While this chapter discusses the legal aspects regarding the distribution of as- sets, other considerations will be discussed in the next chapters, as this is one of the most important and also controversial parts of the dissolution process. A museum's assets can include cash or stocks and bonds; tangible property such as buildings, vehicles, office furniture and equipment, tools, and books; and also *intangible* property such as databases, mailing lists, reproduction rights, copyrights to books, photographs, or intellectual property. Legal documents will be involved such as contracts, bequests, property deeds, and trademark registrations. One of the reasons to prepare a Plan of Dissolution early is to ensure that the museum has a comprehensive and up-to-date inven- tory of all assets that include any requisite ownership documents, provenance,

Figure 2.1.   Public Memorial Service for the Corcoran Gallery of Art, September 27, 2014. Photograph by John Punsalan

values, and location. If this inventory is not ready at the time of dissolution, it is a time-consuming process that will require staff to focus only on this task, thereby delaying the dissolution process. Some assets may also require new appraisals, which could entail additional time and expense. A museum's permanent collection is its most valuable asset and should already be inventoried with all this detailed information. In addition to a database or digital files, a hard copy will likely be needed for filing purposes.

We have described how a museum's disposal of assets is regulated by the Attorney General and Secretary of State (or other state agency), however a museum's tax-exempt status also brings in the Financial Accounting Standards Board (FASB). This is the independent, nonprofit organization that establishes generally accepted accounting standards and principles in the United States for public and private companies, and nonprofit organizations. The FASB exempts museums from recognizing donations of objects as revenue and capitalizing them, as long as the museum meets standards recognized by the American Alliance of Museums (AAM), which includes using the proceeds from the sale for acquisitions for the collection and direct care of existing collections. Even if a museum sells just part of its collection for operating expenses, then the FASB could determine that the entire collection is a financial asset, which would require museums to regularly establish and update the fair market value for each item. AAM declares under its Ethics, Standards, and Professional Practices that "this action by one museum could jeopardize the FASB exception for all museums."[20]

An important distinction must be made here between distribution, disposal, and deaccession. *Distribution* is a legal term used by the IRS when discussing 501(c)(3) organizations: "Assets of an organization must be permanently dedicated to an exempt purpose. This means that should an organization dissolve, its assets must be distributed for an exempt purpose described in this chapter, or to the Federal Government or to a state or local government for a public purpose."[21] Stephen K. Urice, director of the Project for Cultural Heritage Law & Policy and a professor at the University of Miami School of Law, describes *deaccessioning* as the "permanent removal of a work that previously had been accessioned into a museum's collection pursuant to action of a museum's governing board." He further describes *disposal* as "the manner in which legal title is transferred from the museum to the successor title holder, if there is one."[22] While deaccession can become a public and volatile matter, particularly with high profile works, what is of most concern is the particular method of disposal and the application of the sales proceeds. Deaccessioning is a standard and generally accepted practice for museums, especially when museums change their thematic focus such as with the Albright-Knox Art Gallery in Buffalo, New York, and the Walker Art Center in Minneapolis, Minnesota. Museum advisor Martin Gammon (2018) distinguishes between storage and trophy deaccessions, with the former representing the regular practice and the latter, those important and valuable objects that bring public attention and often disapproval.

These three terms have very different legal meanings and follow very different procedures and requirements, yet they all compel museums to go beyond the laws in order to consider ethics, best practices, and even public relations. *How* assets are distributed, disposed of, and deaccessioned will determine the public benefit and whether the public trust is respected. There have been a number of highly controversial incidents with public protests, board resignations, and withdrawals of donations because this process was neither transparent nor "consistent with the established standards of a museum's discipline" (AAM Code of Ethics). Dissolution is the most drastic change a nonprofit organization can undertake, so it would be appropriate for the board to consider alternatives that would meet the museum's needs short of dissolution. Disposal and deaccessioning are steps that museums sometimes take to avoid closure, especially during a crisis when restrictions on the use of sales proceeds are relaxed.[23] Chapter 4 on Planning for Closure will address some of these closure alternatives with insightful case studies, and the next chapter will discuss ways in which museums can provide a public benefit and remain a trusted institution, even when facing closure.

NOTES

1. Go to www.NOLO.com for a summary of "How to Dissolve a Nonprofit Corporation" in all fifty states, mostly focusing on voluntary dissolutions. NOLO began publishing do-it-yourself legal guides in 1971 and has become one of the leading legal websites.

2. Una Jost (California Attorney & Counselor-at-Law at Jost Legal), in discussion with the author, September 30, 2020.

3. ProPublica, "Nonprofit Explorer," accessed November 24, 2020, https://projects .propublica.org/nonprofits/ctypes.

4. Internal Revenue Service, "Exemption Requirements—501(c)(3) Organizations," accessed November 24, 2020, https://www.irs.gov/charities-non-profits/charitable-organizations/exemption-requirements-501c3-organizations.

5. Internal Revenue Service, "Tax Exempt Status for Your Organization," Publication 557, February 6, 2020, 22, https://www.irs.gov/pub/irs-pdf/p557.pdf.

6. Ibid., p. 25.

7. Don Fullerton, "Tax Policy Towards Art Museums," in *The Economics of Art Museums*, edited by Martin Feldstein (Chicago: University of Chicago Press, 1991), 195–236.

8. In 2017, Elizabeth Merritt wrote a blog post in two parts about Benefit Corporations and B Corps to explore different business models for museums. She describes these as a "hybrid legal structure for mission-driven for-profits" and a "certification program that measures their impact on the world." American Alliance of Museums, Center for the Future of Museums Blog, June 13, 2017, and June 15, 2017, https://www.aam-us.org/2017/06/13/companies-with-benefits-part-1-benefit-corporations/ and https://www.aam-us.org/2017/06/15/companies-with-benefits-part-2-b-corps-or-not-b-corps-that-is-the-question/.

9. Internal Revenue Service, "Suggested Language for Corporations and Associations (per Publication 557)," accessed December 5, 2020, https://www.irs.gov/charities-non-profits/suggested-language-for-corporations-and-associations.

10. The referenced provision of Section 5132 involves the situation where the charter of a subordinate corporation is taken away by or revoked by the organization that granted it.

11. Public Counsel, January 2017, "Guide for the Dissolution of California Nonprofit Public Benefit Corporations," Community Development Project, 14, http://www.publiccounsel.org/tools/publications/files/0243.pdf.

12. Ohio Laws and Rules, Ohio Administrative Code, Title XVII, Corporations-Partnerships, Chapter 1702: Nonprofit Corporation Law, "1702.47 Voluntary dissolution," http://codes.ohio.gov/orc/1702.47.

13. The 192nd General Court of the Commonwealth of Massachusetts, "Section 11A: Dissolution; voluntary; charitable," accessed September 8, 2020, https://malegislature.gov/Laws/GeneralLaws/PartI/TitleXXII/Chapter180/Section11A.

14. The Law Project, May 2013, "Dissolution of Illinois Not for Profit Corporations," https://static1.squarespace.com/static/5871061e6b8f5b2a8ede8ff5/t/592f300e 579fb3cc2a2e0f89/1496264721296/Dissolution-Guide-Illinois_Nonprofits.pdf.

15. Jost, September 30, 2020.

16. Mass.gov, "Guide: Dissolving a Charity," accessed September 6, 2020, https://www.mass.gov/guides/dissolving-a-charity.

17. This was an idea that I came up with for the Pasadena Museum of California Art since, on the final date of operations, when all staff were terminated, storage of items was uncertain because the museum founder/board member/owner had placed the museum and office buildings up for sale, and had removed all museum items from an offsite storage unit that he also owned. Everything worked out well, as the Attorney General approved the transfer of assets.

18. Florida Department of State, Division of Corporations, "E-File Articles of Dissolution," accessed September 8, 2020, https://dos.myflorida.com/sunbiz/manage-business/dissolve-withdraw-business/efile-corporation-dissolution/.

19. ___Mass.gov, "Guide: Dissolving a Charity."

20. American Alliance of Museums, "Ethics, Standards and Professional Practices: Questions and Answers about Selling Objects from the Collection," accessed September 13, 2020, https://www.aam-us.org/programs/ethics-standards-and-professional-practices/questions-and-answers-about-selling-objects-from-the-collection/.

21. Internal Revenue Service, "Tax Exempt Status for Your Organization," Publication 557.

22. University of Miami School of Law, November 19, 2020, "Deaccessioning in American Museums Today," presented by Hoffman Forum, Civil Conversations Program, virtual conference, https://www.youtube.com/watch?v=g2sF3_udGAI.

23. In a press release dated April 15, 2020, the Board of Trustees of the Association of Art Museum Directors passed a series of resolutions in response to the COVID-19 pandemic (https://aamd.org/for-the-media/press-release/aamd-board-of-trustees-approves-resolution-to-provide-additional). "The resolutions state that AAMD will refrain from censuring or sanctioning any museum—or censuring, suspending or expelling any museum director—that decides to use restricted endowment funds, trusts, or donations for general operating expenses. The resolution also addresses how a museum might use the proceeds from deaccessioned art to pay for expenses associated with the direct care of collections. The resolution does not change AAMD's Professional Practices or any other rules currently in place, but instead effectively places a moratorium on punitive actions through April 10, 2022. AAMD also recognizes that it is not within the Association's purview to approve the redirection of restricted funds. However, it hopes that these resolutions will serve as an endorsement to donors or the relevant legal authorities, encouraging them to permit the temporary use of these funds for unrestricted needs."

3

Above and Beyond

Above and beyond the legal requirements for dissolution lie other considerations that museum leaders must be aware of and openly discuss. Many would describe these as ethical or moral, but I prefer to focus on responsibility. This not only responds to museums' *legal* responsibilities as we have just described (being a public benefit corporation) but directs these conversations back to the museums' mission and values, and their crucial role as *social* and *cultural* institutions to discuss additional responsibilities that go one-step further. You will understand what that necessary *one-step* is as you take the time to go through these questions and cases. They will serve as a framework for conversations that must take place at Board of Directors' meetings, senior staff meetings, all-staff meetings, and perhaps even with community groups and donors. Find a good facilitator for these discussions, either internal or external to your museum, and make them part of your regular planning process regardless of where you are with closing. Talk about some of these questions over dinner with your family, over coffee with your colleagues and friends; open yourself up to other points of view and start to articulate your own beliefs. Ideally, you should have these discussions well in advance of the final resolution to dissolve when you are not in full crisis mode. However, if you only have a two-hour board meeting to go through everything, choose carefully which questions and issues you will bring to that critical discussion.

Social and cultural responsibilities will be discussed here within the institutional structure of the museum, but remember that they never cease to exist also on the personal level. You are reading this book alone, your thoughts are your own before you share them, and your actions—or inactions—are yours alone. We cannot completely extricate individual responsibility because individuals—and groups of individuals—form the basis of all societies and cultures. Over the last few decades museums have become integral parts of their societies in partnership with local schools, libraries, and social service organizations. They have a greater awareness of social issues and needs, offering blood drives and voter registration drives, yoga classes and family days, bringing in representatives from different community groups. Cultural awareness, however, came much later to museums. What was once thought to be of concern only to cultural- or ethnic-specific museums is now relevant to all museums that strive for greater cultural inclusion, sensitivity, and competence. We acknowledge today in our wonderfully multicultural world that while societies are comprised of individuals, those individuals have their own cultural backgrounds; they form cultural organizations, and they carry their cultures with them at all times and even passing through generations.

This chapter will address several important issues that must be part of any closure conversation. We start with a brief discussion understanding the relationship between ethics and the law, from ancient Greece to the present day, to introduce the concept of *unwritten* laws and the spirit of the law which go above and beyond our legal requirements as citizens. Having a deep knowledge and respect for the social and cultural norms of our museum communities—*all* the communities that our museums create and belong to—is probably the most important part of a museum closure. Internally we call this our *organizational culture*, which is more than just our mission statement, values, and all our policies and procedures. Diversity and inclusion in museums ensure a greater connection between their internal and external museum communities, and a greater awareness of community norms, histories, beliefs, and priorities. We often claim that museums are one of the most trusted institutions in our society, more than the government, the media, and corporations. Trust entails responsibility to the greater good in the service of society. This very responsibility is the thread that weaves through the seemingly disparate topics in this chapter: community, governance, staff, collections, historic houses, our professional authorities (museum associations), restitution and redistribution, and finally our museum legacy. These are the implications of closing that lie *above and beyond* our written laws, codes, and policies.

ETHICS AND THE LAW

The American Alliance of Museums (AAM) has a professional Code of Ethics for museums (adopted in 1993 and revised in 2000), as does the International Council of Museums and the Association of Art Museum Directors, among many other museum associations that have also released ethics position papers and statements. *Ethics* is the most common way to describe how a museum's staff and directors should "properly" behave according to established industry standards—in addition to legal requirements. However, the term is subjective, often tied to religion and morality, and almost always carries a heavy burden of judgment on both sides (those who must judge and those who have been judged regarding what is ethical). This chapter will not attempt to provide answers about what is ethical or not, nor list all the social and cultural responsibilities of museums, nor even make suggestions about what should or should not be done as best practices, with the exception of the case studies that exemplify a range of museum experiences and choices. We start by examining the AAM Code of Ethics.

> Museums in the United States are grounded in the tradition of public service. They are organized as public trusts, holding their collections and information as a benefit for those they were established to serve. Members of their governing authority, employees and volunteers are committed to the interests of these beneficiaries. The *law* provides the basic framework for museum operations. As nonprofit institutions, museums comply with applicable local, state, and federal *laws* and international conventions, as well as with the specific *legal* standards governing trust responsibilities. This Code of Ethics for Museums takes that compliance as given. But *legal* standards are a minimum. Museums and those responsible for them must do more than avoid *legal* liability, they must take affirmative steps to maintain their integrity so as to warrant public confidence. They must act not only *legally* but also ethically. This Code of Ethics for Museums, therefore, outlines ethical standards that frequently exceed *legal* minimums.[1]

Notice that the words *law* or *legal* appear seven times in this one excerpted paragraph (italics by author). A conversation about ethics, morality, and social responsibility usually starts with the basic legal standards that govern museums as nonprofit corporations, and then goes further. But if we look back at history, we see how complicated this discussion becomes. The ancient Greeks distinguished between written and unwritten laws, noting that man could only change the written laws. *Unwritten laws* were—and continue to be today—understood as customs, traditions, common usage, and also divine and "unshakable" as described by Antigone in Sophocles' play from the fifth century.[2] Then we had the introduction of Christian ethics, and the moral philosophy of the state; then a study of the laws of nature and the laws of physics and the physical world; divine law; and moral law, a construct Immanuel Kant used to describe our conscience. Modern society sees morality and ethics as more separate from government law, which confounds the matter even further. There are times we may choose to break the law when our conscience demands it, or when we are forced to follow a law that we do not believe is fair for the public good, as we see it. For centuries, lawyers and scholars have debated the "letter" and the "spirit" of the law, in which the "spirit" is the interpretation or perceived intention of the "letter" through current social and cultural norms. In the thirteenth century, Thomas Aquinas described law as, "an ordinance of reason for the common good which is promulgated by him who has charge of the community."[3] This statement is important because it possesses three concepts that are crucial to any discussion about museum closures (and purpose and mission): reason, common good, and community. Yet while our laws today carefully consider these three concepts, it is our responsibility to bring them to the fore of every discussion we have surrounding closure so that we follow the unwritten laws as much as the written ones. Museums must have a solid understanding of the social and cultural norms within their communities, as violations of these unwritten standards can be more severe and harder to rectify.

COMMUNITY

It has become popular and easy to throw around the word *community*, enabled by funders who increasingly require evidence of community benefits, service, and participation. By doing so, your museum demonstrates its embrace and inclusion of community, its community-centric mission through community advisory boards, community-based programming, and more. Yet everyone will have a different idea of community because there is no one, overarching community; rather museums have many communities. There is your internal community (staff, volunteers, interns, board, and members); there is the external local community that surrounds your physical museum, your larger museum community of colleagues and partners, your local business community, funding community, cultural community, arts community, and so forth.

When we talk about social responsibility, *society* embraces all these communities and connects them by creating relationships, interactions, and commonalities. Social institutions at all levels (local, state, federal, and even global) are the systems by which individual and communal interests, activities, and needs are served. Museums are considered core social institutions, along with hospitals, churches, schools, and libraries. While we could say that cultural institutions serve specific cultures within society, it is better not to separate them but rather to talk about the institutions and organizations that serve *both* essential social functions and cultural needs at *both* individual and communal levels. Reflect on what community means to your museum. If you believe that your community supports your museum, then identify that community (or communities) at all levels and be specific. How well do you know them and how do you connect with them? Think about your responsibility toward each of these communities.

CASE IN POINT:

Children's Museum of the Sierra, Oakhurst, California

This museum was one of the first of many casualties of COVID-19 when it made a public announcement on April 7, 2020, to close permanently after twenty-three years. Oakhurst is a small city in northern California where tourists stop by on their way to Yosemite. Even with a small staff (one paid full-time and one paid part-time), there was no city support for their annual budget of $55,000, and board members were mostly older. After closing temporarily because of COVID restrictions, their bank account was almost empty, there was no more money coming in (donations or admissions), and they had utility bills due as well as their monthly rent of $2,100. "COVID pushed us over the edge," said volunteer and former board member Gail Lippner.[1] The board realized there was no way to survive, especially as a children's museum, which was one of the last places people would want to take their kids in a pandemic; they just ran out of ideas. Once they made the decision to close, they called the local elementary and middle schools to take their exhibitions for free and also donated items to the organization Fresno Wildlife. They were able to sell some equipment to a group that is opening a new children's museum in nearby Merced, where they are fortunate to have a very low monthly rent in a building next to the University of California, Merced. Most of the closure expenses were shouldered by the long-time volunteer director Jim Elliot.[2] Despite having their auction items stolen just a few months before they announced the closure, the museum still wanted to give back to its community. This is a case not of a large museum with an equally large and valuable collection but of a small museum in a small town, to remind us that museums of all sizes and types must consider how to best distribute their assets according to their local needs. In July 2020, Laura Huerta Migus, executive director of the Association of Children's Museums, commented on the effect of the pandemic on children's museums. "If they're getting 10 percent or 20 percent of what their previous attendance was, that would be successful at this point. We are very worried that our closure rate overall in the industry might approach 30 percent. When a children's museum goes away, it's not just a fun, beautiful venue that goes away, it's a central community resource."[3] This sentiment was echoed by a longtime Oakhurst community member, "Unfortunately, it was the children of the community who experienced the greatest loss."[4]

NOTES

1. Gail Lippner (former volunteer and board member, Children's Museum of the Sierra, Oakhurst), in discussion with the author, August 20, 2020.
2. Jim Elliot (former director, Children's Museum of the Sierra, Oakhurst), in discussion with the author, August 28, 2020.
3. Neda Ulaby, "So Much For 'Please Touch,' After COVID-19, Kids' Museums Will Be Less Hands-On," *Morning Edition*, National Public Radio, July 1, 2020, accessed July 10, 2020, https://www.npr.org/2020/07/01/881626432/so-much-for-please-touch-after-covid-19-kids-museums-will-be-less-hands-on.
4. Larry Gamble, in discussion with the author, September 28, 2020.

If your museum is in trouble, at what point do you reach out to your community for help, and what do you say? Museums always try to show strength and success to their members and donors to safeguard their continued support, so how and when do you open up with your problems? In those cases where museums have not been transparent about their problems with their local communities, the announcement to close or merge comes as a shock and often causes groups to form in protest and in certain cases to seek assistance from the Attorney General. Local leaders and supporters are quoted in the newspapers as wishing they could have done more to help, wishing they knew the museum was in trouble, and feeling very sad about the closure. The following chapters on planning and step-by-step procedures will provide tips and case studies on how to best work with your communities during a closure. Most importantly, get to know your community well, and make sure to include them in meaningful ways.

GOVERNANCE

Probably the largest burden of responsibility in museums falls on the governing bodies, and the type of governance for each museum will play an important role in closure. "Governance management encompasses setting goals and objectives, determining ethical standards, establishing the intended culture, ensuring compliance, and designing and implementing the governance framework" according to BoardEffect (2019).[4] It is based on systems—creating, implementing, monitoring—that support the goals and duties of governance.

Museum governance usually implies the Boards of Trustees or Directors of the nonprofit, but it could also apply to a parent organization such as a foundation or university; a public agency such as the city, county, or state; or even a for-profit corporation. Sometimes there is a dual system of governance, whereby the museum has a separate nonprofit Board of Directors under a larger entity, thereby having two levels of governance. One example is the Los Angeles County Museum of Art, which has a Board of Trustees under its nonprofit Museum Associates (a tax-exempt organization under 501(c)(3) and also a public charity under 509(a)(2) because it receives one-third or more public support), but for certain matters it is also governed by the Los Angeles County Board of Supervisors. University museums usually have volunteer advisory boards in addition to their legal governing bodies, such as the University of California Board of Regents.

The International Committee on Museums' current definition of museums includes "nonprofit," but the American Alliance of Museums allows for many forms of operation and governance and does not specify. A corporate structure is not necessarily better than a nonprofit one, as we can cite many successful for-profit museums that provide a valuable public benefit on their own. These museums offer engaging exhibitions, education, public programming, and very robust retail operations. A few examples are the International Spy Museum and the Crime Museum in Washington, DC, and the Museum of Sex in New York City. The owners of these museums are clearly concerned with profit, which could easily threaten to close a museum that does not also have a commitment to education, exhibitions, public service, and scholarship. The activities and focus of every museum need to remain closely aligned from top to bottom, which is the responsibility of everyone in leadership positions, including staff and governing bodies.

CASE IN POINT:

Wells Fargo History Museums, United States

On the site in San Francisco where Wells Fargo first opened for business in 1852, the first Wells Fargo History Museum opened in 1927, offering free admission, hands-on exhibitions, and guided tours for schoolchildren. Now with twelve museum branches around the United States, the company suddenly announced in September 2020 its decision to close eleven branches and retain only the San Francisco museum. It is widely known that Wells Fargo has been trying to recover from a fake-accounts scandal that occurred in 2016. A new CEO was brought in at the end of 2019. Chief financial officer John Shrewsberry spoke to investors about the transition in December 2019. "Everything's on the table for consideration. He's certainly not beholden to decisions that we made previously."[1] The only reason that Wells Fargo gave for the museum closures is that the decision was *not* related to budget issues. In 2018, the Wells Fargo Regional Foundation gave away $314.8 million in charitable donations for "community development, education, and human services" according to its 990 form. The Wells Fargo History Museum was not listed as a recipient in the tax return, leading one to assume that the museums are part of the corporate structure and not a separate 501(c)(3), since no public tax statements were identified for the museum either. The official memo of the closure included a statement from Ms. Kathy Senior, vice president of strategy and customer experience at Wells Fargo, stating that parts of the collection will be donated to charities, museums, and schools. What is not known is whether each museum collection will stay within those same communities, be transferred to the remaining San Francisco museum, be placed in corporate storage, or sold.

NOTE

1. "Wells Fargo's Scharf Sows Unease while Considering Change," *American Banker*, December 27, 2019, accessed September 16, 2020, https://www.americanbanker.com/articles/wells-fargos-scharf-sows-unease-while-considering-change.

A legal board assumes certain legal responsibilities, as the nonprofit organization is established under the legal guidelines of the Secretary of State and the Internal Revenue Service, which ensures that nonprofits follow guidelines for allowing tax-deductible donations and in declaring any eligible taxes. The Attorney General is charged with "investigating and, when necessary, initiating legal actions against charitable organizations; overseeing nonprofits during mergers, conversions and acquisitions; and reviewing actions taken by executors and trustees where a will or trust contains a charitable gift."[5] The National Council of Nonprofits lists the three primary legal—*fiduciary*—

duties of any corporation, including museums as nonprofit 501(c)(3) corporations:

1. Duty of Care: Take care of the nonprofit by ensuring prudent use of all assets, including facility, people, and good will;
2. Duty of Loyalty: Ensure that the nonprofit's activities and transactions are, first and foremost, advancing its mission; Recognize and disclose conflicts of interest; Make decisions that are in the best interest of the nonprofit corporation; *not in the best interest of the individual board member* (or any other individual or for-profit entity).
3. Duty of Obedience: Ensure that the nonprofit obeys applicable laws and regulations; follows its own bylaws; and that the nonprofit adheres to its stated corporate purposes/mission.[6]

Board members assume these legal duties, and as such, they can be held legally responsible, which is why it is important for boards to establish systems, record their proceedings, and protect themselves individually for liability. Directors & Officers Insurance is paid by the organization to protect individual board members and executive staff if they are sued for a breach of fiduciary duty or for any actual or alleged mismanagement or gross negligence. It can also protect these individuals during a bankruptcy, protecting their personal assets from creditors, past investors, or trustees. Numerous states also provide liability "shields" or "qualified immunity" for uncompensated directors and officers of nonprofit corporations. Nevertheless, there are exclusions to all this protection: if the courts find individuals guilty of fraud, if the conduct is "willful or wanton," or other actions that litigators refer to as "piercing the corporate veil." Regarding dissolution, Public Counsel (2017, 2) states that, "As long as the winding up process is carried out with the requisite exercise of fiduciary duty by the Board of Directors and in accordance with the law, the individual directors will be afforded protection from personal liability in carrying out the dissolution."

We have clearly laid out the importance of strict adherence to legal requirements, organizational procedures, and formalities, in addition to complete transparency and documentation. After that, take *one-step* further to consider the larger responsibility that governing bodies have to benefit the public, which includes their museum communities, societies, and cultures. Make sure to regularly review your foundational documents (Bylaws, Articles of Incorporation, all policies, and any other historical documents).

What is the mission of the museum?
Who does the museum serve?

How does it do this best?
What is the public benefit of the museum, and has it changed over time?
What was the original intent of the museum's incorporation?

These questions will guide your planning process in discussing various scenarios, alternative closures, and even the dissolution itself with the dispersal
of your collection and assets. All your deliberations about closure should be
well documented in the official board meeting minutes to demonstrate that
the board has reviewed other options and has no choice but to close. Remember that the board not only oversees the financial and legal aspects of the
museum but also has oversight of management in general, which means that
the board cannot leave all the internal management decisions to the executive director/CEO, especially during a crisis. The board has a duty to provide
guidance and advice, and to support the executive director by ensuring that
there are enough resources to do their job. Board committees often have the
strongest connections with senior staff and can effectively listen, learn, and
provide support to them.

STAFF

When museum leadership deliberates about closing, oftentimes they leave
out the human element. Discussions focus on finances, legal requirements,
properties, contractual obligations, and so forth. The human element can be
the most difficult to understand because it is hard to quantify and is only su-
perficially reported on spreadsheets. In many small museums, most—if not
all—of the staff are volunteers, with that one paid staff person who devotes
every waking moment to the museum. In these cases, the board is responsible
for the well-being of the staff and volunteers and must make the extra effort
to provide support.

How will a closure affect your museum staff? Volunteers and interns?
Are you including staff in your closure discussions?
How transparent are you with staff about the museum's difficult position?
How well do you know your staff?

Sometimes managers are hesitant about asking probing personal questions
of staff, fearing that they may cross the line and be perceived as creating a
hostile work environment—or worse, that their questions may be interpreted
as inappropriate or even as harassment. Personal information can be used to
determine which staff are the first to be laid off and which ones stay working

until the very end. These difficult decisions start with the tasks that need to be completed and job descriptions, but then other factors enter the discussion. How long has this person worked at the museum? Perhaps they are a single mother who cannot afford to lose the job or maybe they just came back from a medical leave. Are they related to a major donor? Are they cheerful and cooperative or do they always complain and need extra supervision? Senior staff usually have the answers to these questions, which is why it is critical to include senior staff in all closure planning discussions and procedures with the board and attorney, with the intent of making this transition less difficult and protecting the museum from any potential claims of discrimination. Remember that a museum closure will affect everyone differently.

When considering closure, it is also important to reflect on the recent wave of unionizations that have taken place in museums across the United States, currently over twenty of all types and sizes. Mostly front-end workers (part-time and full-time, permanent, and temporary) in visitor services and retail have initiated these actions. They seek a living wage and greater pay equity, but they also seek better working conditions, workplace safety, and a voice at the table. Unionized staff report that they feel undervalued by senior leaders, underpaid, powerless to speak or act effectively, and that they have no job security. When there are layoffs and staff are rehired, unionized employees can participate in these decisions. The same happens when there is a crisis in

Figure 3.1. Marciano Foundation workers protest, 2019. Photograph by Cameron Kiszla/Park Labrea News & Beverly Press

leadership (charges of sexual harassment, mismanagement, racial discrimination, ethics violations). Recent activist demands for greater transparency, ethics, and equality in museums have contributed to the growing wave of staff unionizations. One of the union organizers at the Philadelphia Museum of Art (PMA), Sarah Shaw, declared that, "Making changes to hiring practices, employee support and promotion, and pay equity will make our workplace more diverse and look more like the city of Philadelphia. That is going to make the PMA a more welcoming place to everyone."[7] She believes that a unionized workforce benefits the museum community, meaning both the outside one as well as its employees. Unionizing, in short, is perceived to ensure that promises are kept. It is also seen as a way to change a business model that too often privileges collections and buildings over the people who keep them in good condition and ensure that they remain publicly accessible.[8]

A museum's responsibility toward its staff must be consistent during times of regular operation as well as during times of crisis and closure. If your museum culture is more democratic—perhaps with a smaller staff, a director with an open-door policy, and an emphasis on transparency and good staff/board relations—then you may consider involving staff early in closure deliberations, and perhaps not just senior staff but the entire staff. Your responsibility to inform and prepare staff early, however, must be balanced with the

CASE IN POINT:

The Marciano Art Foundation, Los Angeles, California

In 2012, Maurice and Paul Marciano established the Maurice and Paul Marciano Art Foundation as a 501(c)(3), and a year later purchased the 55,000-square-foot former Scottish Rite Masonic Temple on Wilshire Boulevard for $8 million and had it renovated for millions more. The Marciano Art Foundation opened in May 2017 with the 1,500-piece contemporary art collection of Maurice and Paul Marciano, cofounders of Guess, on loan to the Foundation. The Marciano brothers never hired a permanent curator or an executive director (Maurice's daughter Olivia served as the artistic director), there was no endowment, and the Board of Directors consisted of just the two brothers who covered all operating expenses. Staff complained about low wages (minimum wage of $14.25 in Los Angeles), no benefits, and consistently being told that requests like gallery benches or water were "too expensive or not on budget."[1] Admission was free. On November 1, 2019, 85 percent of the museum's seventy Visitor Service Associates voted to unionize with District Council 36 of the American Federation of State, County and Municipal Employees (AFSCME). A few days later, they were terminated by the Foundation, without the requisite 60-day written notice before instituting mass layoffs. The workers called this an anti-union tactic, and the next day the Foundation announced that it would close that same month due to low attendance, with no plans to reopen. Since that time, the Union has filed suit against the Foundation for unfair labor practices. The Foundation settled, agreeing to pay each worker about ten weeks of pay (total of $205,481 to the seventy plaintiffs and $70,000 in attorney fees). The Foundation-owned building has been put up for sale for almost $14 million. The media described the closure as "unexpected," "very strange," and "a mystery."[2] Art critic Jori Finkel had harsher words to describe the museum as, "from the start a private collection masquerading as a museum. It was the shell of a museum, the illusion of a museum . . . a pseudo-museum."[3] Echoing this sentiment, art critic Carolina Miranda wrote in 2019 that, "Collectors can forgo paying taxes on the acquisition of works by donating them to their namesake nonprofit foundation. That foundation is then exempted from paying taxes. In the meantime, the public display of a collector's art has the potential to make that work—and work the collector may hold privately—much more valuable."[4]

NOTES

1. Stacy Perman, "Inside the Marciano Art Foundation's Spectacular Shutdown," *Los Angeles Times*, February 16, 2020, accessed February 20, 2020, https://www.latimes.com/entertainment-arts/story/2020-02-16/la-et-cm-marciano-art-foundation-story-behind-the-closure.

2. Ibid.

3. Jori Finkel, "The Marciano Masquerade Is Exposed: The Art Foundation, Which Has Closed its Doors, Was Never More than the Shell of a Museum," *Art Newspaper*, November 19, 2019, accessed September 11, 2020, https://www.theartnewspaper.com/comment/comment-or-the-marciano-masquerade-is-exposed.

4. Carolina A. Miranda, "What's Next for Nonprofit Museums after the Closing of the Marciano Art Foundation?," *Los Angeles Times*, November 8, 2019, accessed September 25, 2020, https://www.latimes.com/entertainment-arts/story/2019-11-08/marciano-art-foundation-closing-fallout-museum-union-drive.

responsibility to manage the public disclosure and to properly communicate with museum funders or potential funders. The more these discussions are shared internally, the greater the risk of leaking information before you are ready.

COLLECTIONS

The previous chapter discussed the legal requirements for distribution of collections, and the following chapter will discuss ways to plan for the collection, so here we can focus on other considerations. It is hard to disassociate the legal responsibilities of collections from social and cultural implications. Museums that are incorporated as 501(c)(3) corporation with tax-exempt status must provide a *public benefit*, which forms the core of ethics statements from AAM (public service, public trusts, public confidence) and the International Council of Museums ("in trust for the benefit of society and its development"). The American Association for State and Local History (AASLH) also states that, "In deciding how to dispose of an object, historical organizations must keep in mind that those objects are held in the public trust and that public perception may be more binding than legal or ethical requirements."[9] Donors expect museums to care for their collections in perpetuity, but it is "just incredibly unrealistic" explains Dr. Robert Janes (2009), as few donors include sufficient funding with their material gifts to provide for their long-term maintenance.[10] Museum collections continue to grow, building more storage is expensive, and donors want their works on display.

Most museums have Collections Management policies that designate proceeds from any sales to cover only new acquisitions, and perhaps collections care and management. The courts can also approve a sale to pay creditors or in a bankruptcy proceeding. Even so, *how* a museum sells its collection is an equally important consideration. An auction is the best way to ensure public benefit, as it is publicly accessible and transparent, but the buyers could be private collectors and foundations as well as museums. Museums can also work directly with private dealers to sell pieces to specific museums. When works are bought by private collectors, often it is unknown whether those collectors will make the works publicly accessible to museums, unless stipulated by the museums as conditions for the sale.

It is universally accepted that regardless of the museum's situation or fate, collections must continue to be preserved and well cared for, be publicly accessible, and benefit society, yet this is precisely where opinions diverge, and problems arise. For example, the debate over the Parthenon Marbles between the Greek and British governments centers around not only how the

British government acquired the ancient treasures in the early 1800s but on how many people view them in the British Museum and how well they are preserved "for future generations." Even exhibiting them in the Acropolis Museum in Athens, some argue, would not place them in their original context as part of the adjacent open-air Parthenon.

There is a similar debate surrounding the repatriation of works acquired during colonial and imperialist times. The tides have been turning toward supporting the return of works. In 2017, French president Emmanuel Macron pledged to return all works of African heritage in French museums over the next five years,[11] and in 2018, the leader of Britain's opposition Labour Party Jeremy Corbyn pledged to return the Parthenon Marbles to Greece if he is elected prime minister.[12] Numerous large museums in the United States including the J. Paul Getty Museum, the Metropolitan Museum of Art, and the Boston Museum of Fine Arts have returned works proven to have been illegally acquired, as well as Native American objects. Provenance research has become a priority for many museums that is increasingly funded by large foundation grants. Nevertheless, there are problems associated with repatriation, such as identifying the correct recipient. What if the recipient country does not have a museum or the museum does not have adequate conditions? What if the present-day country does not reflect the culture(s) that first created and used these objects, or if there are conflicting factions within those cultures and countries?

Museums that sell their collections (or partial collections) justify their decision as being in the best interest of the museum, which will benefit the public. The greater good, as many argue, is saving the museum so that it can continue to serve the public through exhibitions and public programs, and by caring for the rest of their collection. One example is the famous case in 2017 of the Berkshire Museum in Pittsfield, Massachusetts, that sold twenty-two significant works from its permanent collection in order to raise funds for building repairs and renovations, operations, and endowment. After two lawsuits to stop the sale and vehement protests and sanctions from the museum field, including the Association of Art Museum Directors and the Massachusetts Cultural Council, the Massachusetts Attorney General agreed to allow the museum to sell up to forty works of art for a maximum total of $55 million. Fifty million dollars of the proceeds could be unrestricted funds, but anything beyond that ($3.25 million) must be allocated for acquisitions and collections maintenance. The museum justified the sale by saying that it was indeed for public benefit. "We are moving forward having secured the future of this museum for generations to come," Elizabeth "Buzz" McGraw, the president of the Berkshire Museum's Board, said in a statement."[13] Executive director Van Shields added, "I'm in this business to transform lives. It is not about what we have. It is about who are we for."[14] Another well-known example is the Delaware Art Museum in 2014 that sold art from its permanent collection to repay its $19.8 million construction debt (from a museum expansion in 2005) and add $10 million to its endowment. Despite similar protests and sanctions, museum CEO Mike Miller stated, "The board felt it was more important to keep this place open for the community than not to sell art."[15]

CASE IN POINT:

Detroit Institute of Arts, Detroit, Michigan

When the City of Detroit declared bankruptcy in December 2013, it wanted to sell the collection of the Detroit Institute of Arts, which was owned by the city since 1919 and originally incorporated as the Detroit Museum of Art in 1885. In a 1997 Operating Agreement, the City designated the Founders Society to raise funds and manage the collection and museum, but the City retained ownership of everything. The collection was appraised at between $2.8 and $4.6 billion (even though it would probably sell for only $1.1 to $1.8 billion). Christie's valued just the works bought with public funds and donated by individuals at between $454 and $867 million.[1] The City's new emergency manager told the museum that it would have to contribute at least $500 million to help pay the City's debts, even if it meant selling its paintings. Faced with this crisis, the museum was able to save its collection by raising $800 million in just two years with what was called the "Grand Bargain." It raised $200 million from the state of Michigan, $330 million from nine major philanthropic foundations, and the rest from local automobile corporations and international donors. As part of the agreement, most importantly, the museum would gain legal title to its building free and clear, as well as the art collection and all related assets. An independent charitable trust was created for the people of Michigan to protect the collection "for educational, research and curatorial services." The State of Michigan Attorney General wrote in his opinion that because of the trust, "no piece in the collection may thus be sold, conveyed, or transferred to satisfy city debts."[2] This example demonstrates how the museum was able to secure the future of its collection—and the entire museum—by having already established good will and trust with its local and national foundations, corporate funders, and the community of Detroit who all rallied together quickly to support the museum and establish proper legal protections for the future.

NOTES

1. David Ng, "Detroit Institute of Arts Collection Worth Billions, Report Says," *Los Angeles Times*, July 11, 2014, accessed September 12, 2020, https://www.latimes.com/entertainment/arts/culture/la-et-cm-detroit-institute-of-arts-20140711-story.html.
2. Bill Schuette, "Opinion #7272 of the State of Michigan Attorney General's Office," Stropheus LLC, June 13, 2013, accessed September 23, 2020, https://stropheus.com/museum/dia-deaccessioning/.

A recent trend has seen museums deaccessioning works in the permanent collection to diversify those same collections, acknowledging the lack of women and indigenous artists, and artists of color. Just in the last couple of years, the Baltimore Museum of Art sold seven paintings by white, male artists mostly at auction, earning $7.93 million to purchase works by women and artists of color, and the San Francisco Museum of Modern Art sold a Mark Rothko painting at auction for $50.1 million and bought eleven works by artists of color. The Art Gallery of Ontario in Canada sold twenty paintings to purchase works by indigenous artists, and Everson Museum in Syracuse, New York, sold a Jackson Pollock at auction for $12 million to add works by underrepresented artists. These sales have been generally applauded by the museum community as good intentions to support underrepresented artists (within our current social climate of diversity and inclusion), except when works are taken out of the public realm or when the transactions are not publicly disclosed. Other concerns arise about the true extent of diversity in these museums beyond their collections. How diverse are the acquisitions committees or curatorial leadership, or even the Boards of Directors? One wonders if there are alternatives for this same goal of diversification, and if museums might bypass the market and trade with each other—a white artist for a Black artist, a male artist for a female artist, a Jackson Pollock for a Carlos Almaraz? Unfortunately, an even trade would require placing a value on the works that would make them fungible assets, which is why museums prefer to transfer to other museums and nonprofit organizations with no expectations other than providing public benefits.

PROFESSIONAL AUTHORITY

Museum associations may not have legal power over museums like the Attorney General, Secretary of State, or other public bodies in the United States, but they do hold significant influence in the professional museum field, particularly surrounding accreditation. The sale of works to sustain general museum operations is generally not sanctioned by the AAM, AAMD, and other organizations because it treats the collection as a commodity or a financial asset at the expense of long-term interests. The Museums Association (MA) of Great Britain provides guidelines and toolkits on disposing of items from a museum collection, both curatorially and financially motivated. The toolkits are especially helpful for identifying ethical criteria for the disposal. After reviewing these documents and contacting the Museums Association, Arts Council England, or whichever organization has conferred accreditation, British museums are required to submit a *Compliance Report for Financially Motivated Disposal of Items from a Museum Collection*. Some of the questions on the form are helpful for conversations around the disposal of assets.

> How will the proposed disposal significantly improve the long-term public benefit derived from the remaining collection, and how will the proposed disposal serve the long-term local and general public interest?
>
> The proposed disposal should not be to generate short-term revenue; please outline how the proceeds from the sale will be used.
>
> Please outline how the proposed disposal is a last resort after other sources of funding have been thoroughly explored.
>
> What extensive prior consultation with sector bodies has been taken?
>
> How have the views of stakeholders and those who have a vested interest in a proposed disposal been sought (for example, donors, researchers, local and source communities, and others served by the museum)?[16]

The Compliance Report is used by the Museums Association to decide whether the proposed sale meets the requirements of its Code of Ethics and the Accreditation Standard. Interestingly, the MA notes that it will keep its review process and advice confidential, unless the museum brings the matter of its proposed sale into the public domain. If it does, then the MA will "publish its advice in the interests of transparency and accountability." The process takes several months, requiring the Ethics Committee to meet and decide if there are any impacts on accreditation status.

The American Alliance of Museums does not have a process like the MA that requires official approval of selling assets. Julie Hart, senior director of Museum Standards & Excellence at AAM explained that, "We do encourage

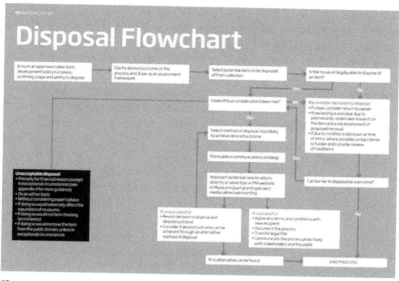

Figure 3.2.   Disposal Flowchart from the Disposal Toolkit. Courtesy of the Museums Association. (www.museumsassociation.org)

museums to reach out to give us the head's up before taking major action. This gives us the opportunity to offer guidance or share any potential concerns we see. This is particularly important for accredited museums, so we don't have to intervene, apply probation, or possibly remove accreditation after-the-fact."[17] AAM has a document called *Direct Care of Collections: Ethics, Guidelines, and Recommendations*, which does not address the legal dispersal of collections. AAM offers useful resources on its website under Ethics, Standards and Best Practices,[18] including a comprehensive compilation of ethical codes, statements, and guidelines from the following organizations: Alliance Professional Networks, Association of Art Museum Curators, Association of Art Museum Directors, American Association for State and Local History, American Institute for Conservation of Historic and Artistic Works, Association of Zoos and Aquariums, International Council of Museums, Museum Store Association, National Council on Public History, American Anthropological Association, American Educational Research Association, American Institute of Architects, American Library Association, Archaeological Institute of America, Association of Fundraising Professionals, Association of Independent Information Professionals, e-Philanthropy Foundation, and the Giving Institute.

At the beginning of the COVID-19 pandemic, the Association of Art Museum Directors (AAMD) issued a press release on April 15, 2020, relaxing its stance on restricted uses of funds in museums.[19] "AAMD will not impose censure or sanctions on an institution that considers the following sources for general operations, including necessary expenses such as staff compensation and benefits: the income (not principal) from funds generated by deaccessioned works of art, regardless of when the works were deaccessioned." Christine Anagnos, AAMD executive director, further states that, "We recognize the severity of the current crisis and the immediate financial needs of many institutions. At the same time, whether it is the principal of an endowment or the art that comprises a museum's collection, we need to protect important assets for future use"[20]—the argument here being that it is better to sacrifice a small part of collections and museums to protect the whole and sustain history and legacy. The president of AAMD, Brent Benjamin, affirmed that this is a "crisis without precedent in our lifetime." Without professional restrictions during this current crisis, it is incumbent on each museum to determine the "greater good" and how best to serve the public. Yet even after the pandemic crisis is over and restrictions are put back in place, there will inevitably be more unexpected crises. Professional museum associations are there to support and guide museums through any crisis, and museums should always heed their directives and seek their guidance. However, the museum field is incredibly large and diverse, and in taking *one-step* further, museums must also consider their own most responsible path forward.

REDISTRIBUTION OF WEALTH

Museums are always raising money, both earned income and contributed donations that will sufficiently cover their expenses, but hardly ever do they think about how to *give away* money. If we switch our discussion to *wealth* instead of money, this statement becomes more relevant to the matter at hand of closure and transition. Joseph Stiglitz, 2001 Nobel laureate in Economic Sciences, explains the difference; "wealth and capital are two distinct concepts; the former reflects control over resources, the latter is a key input into production processes."[21] Wealth incorporates not just cash, but also all assets such as property, collections, and everything that is of value to the organization. We can even include a museum's history, brand, and website if they have value to someone. Therefore, if wealth is about having *control* over your resources, then being responsible requires museums to determine what is within their control (and within the law) to distribute. We assume that discussions of distribution of wealth occur only as a legal requirement for the dissolution of nonprofit organizations with a 501(c)(3), while actually they should be part of any regular planning process that obliges museums to reflect, imagine, and strategize. The matter of distribution, therefore, now becomes a matter *re*distribution. By framing the legal requirement of distribution of assets into a discussion of redistribution, we open the doors to bring in similarly critical and timely questions of restitution, reconciliation, repatriation, and reform.

Are you able to effectively take care of your assets? Are they in a proper storage space?

How often are they viewed, studied, and exhibited by the public?

Do you make your collection available for students and scholars, and is your collection digitized and publicly accessible online for wider access?

What documentation exists for your collection, including how it was acquired?

How do you describe parts of your collection that might be historical, cultural, or religious, and who is responsible for writing those descriptions?

How is your museum and its collection connected with your local or regional community?

Is there a connection with a wider ethnic or tribal group?

Are you aware of any historic injustices that have been committed within your local or regional community; are there current grievances or protests that still happen?

What is your experience with activists?

Who is making these decisions at the museum?

Is there a diversity of voices and experiences at the table, and what are you doing to reduce implicit or unconscious bias?

Review your mission, your programs, and collections, and think deeply about how it all benefits the public, *who* is the public that is already benefiting, and who *should* benefit more.

Historically, land was redistributed to confront injustices, such as in South Africa with colonialism and apartheid or in Mexico with colonialism and the Catholic Church. The United States government has made reparations with Native Americans, and with Japanese Americans interned during World War II, by offering land and cash. More related to museums is their complicity in the building of collections through colonialism, illegal (or unethical) seizure and plunder, immoral practices such as slavery, and often-illegal archaeological excavations and purchases. This is the reason why, among thousands of other examples, the last Aztec Emperor Moctezuma's great feather headdress sits in the Museum of Ethnology in Vienna, Austria. If you are a small children's museum or a science museum or even a botanical garden, you might ask, how does all this apply to me? By holding assets—the donations your museum receives, property, collections of any size or type—in the public trust, museums have a social and cultural responsibility to address historic and current issues of inequity and injustice. Museums control all the wealth that they have accumulated and carefully maintain, and they must always weigh that control in the best public interest.

When charitable foundations operate museums, there exists an additional responsibility to benefit the public through the foundation's grant-making activities. Whether it is a family foundation, corporate foundation, or community foundation, the IRS defines *charitable* as:

> relief of the poor, the distressed, or the underprivileged; advancement of religion; advancement of education or science; erection or maintenance of public buildings, monuments, or works; lessening the burdens of government; lessening neighborhood tensions; eliminating prejudice and discrimination; defending human and civil rights secured by law; and combating community deterioration and juvenile delinquency.[22]

When these types of museums close, foundations may already have plans to disperse the collections and other assets that are part of their museums. Some examples include the McCormick Tribune Foundation that closed the McCormick Freedom Museum in 2010 (read the case study in chapter 4), the Kemp Foundation in Missouri that closed the Kemp Auto Museum in 2015 because of a change in the foundation's focus, and the Annenberg Foundation below that closed its museum in response to COVID-19.

CASE IN POINT:

Annenberg Space for Photography, Century City, California

The Annenberg Space for Photography opened in Century City in Los Angeles in 2009 as an "initiative of the Annenberg Foundation and its Trustees." A family foundation established in 1989, the Annenberg Foundation supports arts and culture, community partnerships, education, and global humanitarianism. It was the only photography museum in Los Angeles, it had free admission, and it presented three exhibitions a year. In June 2020, the Foundation stated on its website that it "will not re-open after closing its doors to the public in mid-March, in order for the Annenberg Foundation to further focus its philanthropy on the coronavirus pandemic recovery. . . . Going forward, the Annenberg Foundation will focus on continuing to offer its support to those affected by the pandemic. In addition, it will look at building out its commitment to social and economic justice issues."[1] Two months later, the Foundation announced a donation of 1,000 photographic prints by about 250 contemporary photographers "from its Annenberg Space for Photography exhibitions" to the Library of Congress, along with photographic prints for long-term preservation from ten other exhibitions hosted at the photography museum, and a $1 million donation. It was unclear whether the collection belonged to the museum or the foundation, and there was no mention of the donation in the closure announcement. Wallis Annenberg (chairman of the board, president and CEO of the Annenberg Foundation) explained, "So even as the Photo Space closes its doors, I feel like we're opening a new one with the Library of Congress and letting even more people experience these stunning images."[2]

NOTES

1. "Annenberg Space for Photography to Close Its Doors After a Decade of Bringing Groundbreaking Exhibitions and Visual Storytelling to the Los Angeles Community," Annenberg Foundation, Annenberg Now (blog), June 8, 2020, https://annenberg.org/annenberg-now/annenberg-space-for-photography-to-close-its-doors-after-a-decade-of-bringing-groundbreaking-exhibitions-and-visual-storytelling-to-the-los-angeles-community/.
2. Brett Zongker, "Two Major Gifts to Reimagine Visitor Experience and Enhance Photography Collections at Library of Congress," Library of Congress, News from the Library of Congress, August 6, 2020, accessed September 12, 2020, https://www.loc.gov/item/prn-20-051/two-major-gifts-to-

Organizations like the AAMD and AAM recommend transferring or dispersing collections to accredited museums that can best provide for their care, however this excludes many community-based museums, tribal museums, and ethnic-specific museums that may have adequate facilities but choose not to become accredited. Museums might consider an exchange of collections that would not only diversify both museums but also create long-term partnerships. This may not be applicable to museums that are permanently closing, but it could be useful in considering various closure alternatives, and even in thinking about how your receiving nonprofit organization will best

use and care for your collection. You may consider placing conditions on your transfer, such as opening access for indigenous works, for restitution of works, and even allowing for exchanges with community-based museums.

CASE IN POINT:

Yale Union Center for the Arts, Portland, Oregon

In 2018, leaders at Yale Union started noticing gentrification happening in their Portland neighborhood and thought about how they could respond to this, pondering different models of restorative social change. Former executive director Yoko Ott proposed a land and building transfer to the Native Arts and Cultures Foundation (NACF), based in Vancouver, Washington. Yale Union's 30,000-square-foot building dates to 1908 and is listed on the National Register of Historic Places. Yale Union did not have a permanent collection, but it had a large art library, published ten books, and owned its building that was valued at $5 million. They had also spent over $7 million renovating the building. Commenting on this radical decision, Yale Union's board president and cofounder Aaron Flint Jamison states, "Having been able to fulfill our mission through the unearned privilege of property ownership, it's now time that we hand over the keys!" He emphasizes that this was not a gift or donation, but a *transfer of ownership*. The Native Arts and Culture Foundation will move to Portland and establish its new national headquarters as the Center for Native Arts and Cultures. They will continue to serve the local community of Portland as a site of contemporary artistic and cultural production, local partnerships, and a gathering space for Indigenous artists and cultural ceremonies. NACF President/CEO Lulani Arquette talks about this transformative opportunity, saying that they "stand united with all to reclaim Native truth, engage anti-racism, and address important issues we face today."[1] Jamison further confirms that the land deed and title have a "restrictive covenant" that allows the space to be used only for art and culture presentation, which was important to keep away real estate developers and gentrification.[2] "What does it mean to have radical acts of imagination around restoration with Indigenous communities?" asks Seattle conceptual artist C. Davida Ingram. "It's exciting to think, so what else is possible?"[3]

NOTES

1. "Native Arts and Cultures Foundation to Gain Ownership of Yale Union Building in Historic Repatriation of Property; After One Decade, Yale Union to Dissolve in 2021," Native Arts and Cultures Foundation, Press Release, July 16, 2020, https://www.nativeartsandcultures.org/media-kit.

2. Brian Oaster, "With the Transfer of Yale Union Building to Native Ownership, a Hub for Indigenous Artists is Born," *Street Roots*, July 22, 2020, accessed September 20, 2020, https://www.streetroots.org/news/2020/07/22/transfer-yale-union-building-native-group-hub-indigenous-artists-born.

3. Naomi Ishisaka, "Arts Organization Yale Union Transfers its Land and Building to Native Ownership," *Seattle Times*, July 21, 2020, https://www.seattletimes.com/entertainment/arts-organization-yale-union-transfers-its-land-and-building-to-native-ownership/.

If your museum has significant assets and you have decided to dissolve, another option is to donate any remaining assets to a legacy community fund, such as establishing a nonprofit fund with the South Dakota Community Foundation (https://sdcommunityfoundation.org/). The Council on Foundations provides information on community foundations that "play a key role in identifying and solving community problems." The Council's website provides an interactive map of over 750 community foundations in the United States that have been accredited by the National Standards for US Community Foundations.[23]

The UK Equality Act, created in 2010, provides a legal framework to understand the "public sector duty regarding socio-economic inequalities." Section 1 of the Act states: "An authority to which this section applies must, when making decisions of a strategic nature about how to exercise its functions, have due regard to the desirability of exercising them in a way that is designed to reduce the inequalities of outcome which result from socio-economic disadvantage."[24] This Act covers nine protected characteristics: age, disability, gender reassignment, marriage and civil partnership, pregnancy and maternity, race, religion or belief, and sex. Most interesting about this Act is the Public Sector Equality Duty that was added one year later, as Section 149 of the Act. Most museums in the UK are considered public bodies (publicly funded service providers), so this requires the public sector to consider how their decisions and policies affect people with all of these attributes, in addition to those with socioeconomic disadvantages.

MUSEUM LEGACY

In thinking about wealth and public benefit, it comes naturally to think also about legacy. Legacy is more important to some museums than others, and your museum founders may have already included stipulations in your founding documents that ensure a particular legacy by taking certain actions (or prohibiting actions). Other museums may be completely satisfied with how they have served the public for the duration of their operations, with no concern for a post-closure future other than fulfilling all the legal requirements.

What will be the legacy of this museum when it closes or merges?
If there were important founders of the museum or funders that donated land, collections, and more, what will be their legacy?
If your buildings do not remain—the same buildings that prominently list your donors' names—how will your community remember them and what is your responsibility toward them? How closely tied is your legacy to your buildings?

Buildings can be important visual symbols of a museum and its place in society, especially when those buildings are historic, architecturally significant, or centrally located. The University of Chicago report *Set in Stone: Building America's New Generation of Arts Facilities, 1994–2008* (2012) raises ethical considerations about major building projects for museums.

On one hand, the sustainability of cultural organizations and the cultural sector as a whole is important to maintaining the cultural vitality of this country. On the other hand, not everyone believes that maintaining cultural vitality is a priority, and therefore, not everyone believes that the public should have to pay for doing so. These projects take a toll on the organizations themselves, but also on those that help pay for the projects. Not only do wealthy philanthropists sometimes have to see their investments crumble, but taxpayers also have to see their hard-earned money be devoted to failing projects that may not continue to help deliver a public good.[25]

Legally, museums can sell their assets to pay debts or to cover any closure expenses, but whatever is sold cannot constitute "all or substantially all" of the assets or be essential to museum operations. Donor-imposed restrictions that are legally enforceable need to be taken into consideration, as well as whether the museum is a state-chartered institution. Whether these are valuable works of art or office furniture, museums should evaluate if a sale of assets will provide the legacy that they desire, or whether it will cause controversy and bad will in the community and museum field. However, these decisions are first determined by each museum's financial situation, as well as the prevailing approval of the state Attorney General, who also represents the interests of the public.

CASE IN POINT:

Roy Rogers and Dale Evans Museum, California and Missouri

In 1967, the museum opened in Apple Valley in California in an old bowling alley that husband and wife Rogers and Evans purchased and renovated. Nine years later it moved to a larger building in nearby Victorville. Rogers also owned the Roy Rogers Double R Bar Ranch to keep his horses, a few miles away in Oro Grande. Long before this, Roy Rogers bought out the rights to his name and likeness, with the foresight to monetize himself. After Roy Rogers died in 1998, and Dale Evans died in 2001, their oldest son Roy Rogers Jr. (Dusty) dissolved the California nonprofit in 2003 and moved the museum to Branson, Missouri, in the hopes of attracting more tourists. Unfortunately, not enough tourists came and the fanbase was getting older, so in 2009 Dusty made the decision to close the museum. In discussing this decision, Dusty admitted, "Dad always said, 'If the museum is costing you money, then liquidate everything and move on.' Myself and the family have tried to hold together the museum and collection for over 15 years, so it is very difficult to think that it will be gone soon."[1] After the death of Dale Evans, the IRS levied a high tax on the Rogers' estate, and more cash was required to keep the museum open. To pay their debts, the family sold all the collection at auction with Christie's, earning a total of almost $3 million. The Autry Museum of Western Heritage bought several significant pieces from that auction and acquired the Roy Rogers and Dale Evans Archives for its library[2] available for the public to study.[3] Rogers' famous horse Trigger was saved by a group of local developers in Apple Valley, who placed the 24-foot-high statue prominently in the center of town.[4] The Apple Valley Legacy Museum also contains memorabilia of Trigger, Roy Rogers, and Dale Evans, and the current owners of the Double R Bar Ranch built their new fence using lumber from the Victorville museum when it was dismantled. In Rogers' hometown in southern Ohio, there is a Roy Rogers–Dale Evans Collectors Association in Portsmouth, a Roy Rogers Scholarship Fund for a student to attend

Shawnee State University in Portsmouth, Ohio, and an annual Roy Rogers festival held since 1984.

NOTES

1. Sarah Jones, "This is the Truth Behind Why the Roy Rogers Museum Finally Shut its Doors for Good," *Scribol*, February 28, 2020, accessed September 22, 2020, https://scribol.com/lifestyle/money-blunders/roy-rogers -museum-shut-doors/40/.

2. "Autry Acquires the Roy Rogers and Dale Evans Archive Collection to be Made Accessible to Researchers and the Public," GeneAutry.com, News Archive: 2010, May 17, 2010, https://www.geneautry.com/news/2010/rogers -evans-archive.html.

3. Roy Rogers and Dale Evans Archives at the Autry Museum of the American West, http://autry.iii.com/search~S0?/troy+rogers+and+dale+evans/ troy+rogers+and+dale+evans/1%2C5%2C5%2CB/frameset&FF=troy+rogers +and+dale+evans+archive+circa+1920s+2000s+manuscript+collection&1%2 C1%2C.

4. Rene Ray De La Cruz, "Trigger is Back: Statue of Roy Rogers' Beloved Horse Finds New Home at Spirit River Center," *Daily Press*, February 21, 2018, accessed September 22, 2020, https://www.vvdailypress.com/ news/20180221/trigger-is-back-statue-of-roy-rogers-beloved-horse-finds-new -home-at-spirit-river-center.

Museums Can Plan Their Legacy, and Here are a Few Examples to Consider

1. Paper and digital archives of the organization can be donated to academic research institutions or other nonprofit organizations such as a local history museum or municipal museum. This is not so easy, as individual archives are more desirable than organizational archives, unless they are historically significant museums. Museums should consider making a cash donation for archival care if they are in such a position or secure a donation from a board member or outside donor.

2. Archive your website by determining what day it will stop and freeze for online access, negotiate with another institution to maintain your website, especially if it has significant digital resources, or transfer your website to another website (or exiting museum online archive) to either be archived or maintained active. There are important nonprofit digital repositories such as Wikimedia Commons (https://commons

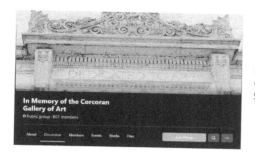

Figure 3.3. Facebook page, In Memory of the Corcoran Gallery of Art. September 15, 2020

.wikimedia.org), and you could contribute content about the history of your museum to Wikipedia (https://www.wikipedia.org). Think about social media—will another institution take over your accounts? Will you archive or transfer the contents? A public Facebook page was created "In Memory of the Corcoran Gallery of Art" in 2014, about one month before the museum closed permanently.[26]

3. Consider what will happen to your name. Will it continue as part of a merger or acquisition? Would you sell your name to another museum that is interested in opening? Whether you remove the building signage depends on if you will sell the building, sublease it, or terminate a lease agreement. Over two years after the Pasadena Museum of California

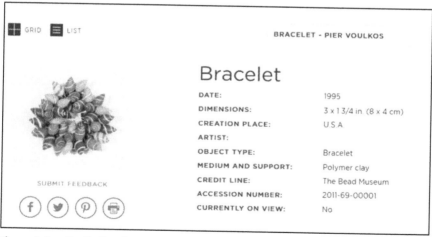

Figure 3.4. Credit line for an object in the permanent collection of the Mingei International Museum in San Diego, California, donated by the Bead Museum in Glendale, Arizona. It closed in 2011 and donated its entire collection of 11,650 beads, beaded objects, and a library, to the Mingei. September 24, 2020[27]

Art closed permanently in 2018 and the building was subsequently sold, the signage still remains high on top of the building.
4. Distributing collections and assets that will live on, cared for by another nonprofit organization. The relevant questions are whether the collection will stay together or be separated, if the collection will remain in the same city or region, and if the collection will be exhibited and used for study and research. Are the receiving organization's values, standards, and operating procedures in alignment with your own? Museums can ensure that distributed collections will retain the original donor recognition in the object labels, as well as the museum name (e.g., Donated by the former Museum of _____).

HISTORIC HOUSE MUSEUMS

There was a time, not too long ago, when many people in the museum and preservation fields were asking if there were just too many house museums. The National Trust for Historic Preservation estimates that there are now more than 15,000 house museums in the United States, many with annual budgets of less than $250,000 (or much less than that), few with endowments, and most run by volunteers or a single staff person.[28] One of the reasons there are so many, according to the National Trust, is the broad definition of historic sites that includes architecturally significant buildings and homes (of all sizes, styles, and time periods) of important people and historic events.[29] The National Trust was chartered by Congress in 1949 but is now a privately funded nonprofit and owns numerous important homes such as Philip Johnson's Glass House, Frank Lloyd Wright's Falling Water, and Mies van der Rohe's Farnsworth House. These are managed by local nonprofit preservation organizations or foundations as an example of co-stewardship. Many historic houses are owned by nonprofit foundations, by the city or state, or by universities. Others are part of museums such as Eero Saarinen's Miller House at the Indianapolis Museum of Art donated by the original owner's children, and the Sheats-Goldstein home that was bequeathed to the Los Angeles County Museum of Art by its owner. When the last owner of the George Wyth House in Iowa died in 1979, she left it to the Cedar Falls Historical Society, stipulating that the house remain a museum for at least thirty years. The Historical Society was unable to keep it operating as a museum because there were not enough return visitors, so they now open the house to the public just for special occasions.

An excerpt from the Statement of Professional Standards and Ethics of the American Association for State and Local History (AASLH) demonstrates

CASE IN POINT:

Finchcocks Musical Museum, Goudhurst, Kent, United Kingdom

Museum founders Richard and Katrina Burnett purchased the historic Georgian manor named Finchcocks, originally built in 1725 and named after the family that lived on the site in the thirteenth century. Richard was a concert pianist and a partner in Adlam Burnett Historical Keyboard Instruments Ltd., which built instruments in a workshop at the residence until 1980. In 1976, after extensive restoration to the home, it opened to the public as the Finchcocks Musical Museum, with the Burnett's private collection of around 115 period keyboard instruments (harpsichords, clavichords, organs, early pianos, and more). The instruments were in full working order, used regularly for performances at the home, recordings, and other public events and educational projects. The museum also had a cellar restaurant, thirteen acres of parkland, and even offered jazz nights. In 1984, the Burnetts created the Finchcocks Charity for Musical Education whose aim was and continues to be "to champion the study and musical use of historical keyboard instruments in bringing to life the sound-world of the great baroque, classical and romantic composers, and to help preserve the vital skills and expertise required to restore and maintain them through training and apprenticeship."[1] It was awarded the Best Musical Museum in England in 2012, but sadly, by 2015 Richard Burnett had become completely deaf. The Burnetts decided to close the museum, sell Finchcocks, and most of their collection. The Richard Burnett Collection of Early Keyboard Instruments sold at auction for a total of £835,462, and the contents of the Finchcocks Musical Museum (paintings and fine art objects) sold for an additional £301,180.[2] Funds from the auction went to the Finchcocks Charity for Musical Education. The Burnetts retained fourteen important original keyboard instruments from their collection, to be available for all musicians to study and give performances at their new home in nearby Kent, England. The sales proceeds maintain these instruments in good condition, and support the continued training of professional restorers and musicians. Finchcocks was sold in 2016 for over $3 million, and the new owners have pledged to continue the Burnetts' commitment to music. They appointed a musical director to select and maintain the instruments at the home, and they offer a series of residential piano courses for all levels as well as musical retreats.

NOTES

1. The Finchcocks Charity, "Charity," accessed September 19, 2020, http://www.finchcocks.co.uk/charity.html.
2. "The Richard Burnett Collection and Contents of Finchcocks Dazzles at Auction," *ArtDaily Newsletter*, accessed September 19, 2020, https://artdaily.cc/news/87241/The-Richard-Burnett-Collection-and-Contents-of-Finchcocks-dazzles-at-auction#.X2b254tlCUk.

that historic house museums must accept the same responsibilities as all museums, in addition to their legal requirement to provide public benefit.[30]

- In fulfillment of their public trust, association members must be responsible stewards, giving priority to the protection and management of the historical resources within their care and preserving the physical and intellectual integrity of these resources.
- The governing authority has the responsibility to safeguard the organization's assets, including, but not limited to: the good name of the organization, its mission, its human and financial resources, collections, facilities, property, members and donors.
- No revenue producing activities should violate or compromise the integrity of an institution's mission. These activities should not hamper the ability of an institution or individual to meet professional standards or endanger an institution's nonprofit status.
- History institutions must respect all legal, ethical, and cultural standards regarding individual privacy, human-based research and access to and use of sensitive cultural materials.
- History organizations exist to serve the public interest and must always act in such a way as to maintain public confidence and trust.

Preservationists usually prefer to save buildings that are historically important at the expense of the museum or nonprofit organization that might own or operate them, and even at the expense of public access. Because land is often more valuable than buildings, historic houses are always in danger of being demolished by real estate developers in private sales where the public may not hear about the sale until too late. Historic tax credits are meant to encourage the rehabilitation of historic buildings, administered by the National Park Service and the Internal Revenue Service together with State Historic Preservation Officers. If a building is on the National Register of Historic Places, it is eligible for a 20 percent tax credit, otherwise a 10 percent credit to subsidize expenses. These tax credits are often used when "repurposing" a historic site.

When house museums find themselves struggling, the AASLH encourages their boards and staff to consider "alternate means for the care and public benefit of its structures and collections," which they say may be unavoidable.[31] One example is when the City of Memphis, Tennessee, sold the James Lee House, which dates from 1853, to private owners that opened a bed-and-breakfast after extensive restoration work. In their Ethics Position Paper #3 (2009), the AASLH lists a page of important questions and issues to address during this process of privatization. Covenants or protective easements can be placed on historical houses before a sale or transfer of ownership to ensure preservation. Richard Moe, president of the National Trust from 1993 to 2009, explains, "Preservation has really evolved over the years to becoming a force for community revitalization, a tool if you will."[32] Most revitalization efforts take place in minority and rural communities, and inner cities, which raises the importance of partnerships at all levels. When a historic house museum closes, transformation or repurposing is made possible through partnerships that ensure the public can continue to appreciate the history and beauty of these important buildings.

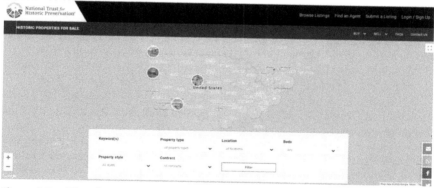

Figure 3.5.   Historic Properties for Sale on the website of the National Trust for Historic Preservation. September 20, 2020[33]

NOTES

1. American Alliance of Museums Code of Ethics, excerpt, emphasis added, https://www.aam-us.org/programs/ethics-standards-and-professional-practices/code-of-ethics-for-museums/.

2. "That you, a mere mortal, could override the gods, the great unwritten, unshakable traditions. They are alive, not just today or yesterday: They live forever, from the first of time, and no one knows when they first saw the light." Sophocles, *Three Theban Plays: Antigone, Oedipus the King, Oedipus at Colonus*, trans. Robert Fagles (New York: Viking, 1984), 17.

3. Saint Thomas Aquinas, *Summa Theologica*. Part I–II (Pars Prima Secundae), trans. Fathers of the English Dominican Province, The Project Gutenberg eBook, XC, Art 4.

4. Lena Eisenstein, "What is Governance Management and Why is it Important?," BoardEffect (blog), November 13, 2019, accessed September 16, 2020, https://www.boardeffect.com/blog/what-governance-management-important/.

5. "About this Site," on James E. Tierney's website StateAG.org, accessed September 16, 2020, https://www.stateag.org/about/this-site.

6. "Board Roles and Responsibilities. Tools & Resources," National Council of Nonprofits, accessed September 16, 2020, https://www.councilofnonprofits.org/tools-resources/board-roles-and-responsibilities.

7. Eric Morse, "Why Employees at the Philadelphia Museum of Art are Unionizing," *Art Museum Teaching*, July 17, 2020.

8. Steve Dubb, "Museum Unions Seek More than Improved Pay, Union Organizers Insist," *Nonprofit Quarterly*, March 3, 2020.

9. Rick Beard, "When a History Museum Closes," American Association for State and Local History, Ethics Position Paper 2 (June 2006): 2.

10. Robert Janes in Amy Rogers Nazarov, "Ethical Considerations for Museum Closures," American Alliance of Museums, Mission & Institutional Planning, July 1, 2009, https://www.aam-us.org/2009/07/01/ethical-considerations-for-museum-closures/. Robert Janes was director of the Glenbow Museum in Calgary, Canada in the 1990s, and then editor in chief of the journal *Museum Management and Curatorship*.

11. Naomi Rea, "France's President Has Promised to Return Africa's Heritage—Now Macron's Pledge Is Being Put to the Test," *Artnet News*, March 8, 2018.

12. Jeremy Corbyn did not become Prime Minister in the December 2019 elections, and on October 29, 2020 he was suspended from the Labour Party over the release of a report by UK's Equality and Human Rights Commission.

13. Andrew Russeth, "Berkshire Museum Completes Controversial, Contested Art Sales, Netting $53.3 M," *ARTNews*, November 27, 2018, accessed September 14, 2020, https://www.artnews.com/art-news/news/berkshire-museum-completes-controversial-contested-art-sales-netting-53-3-m-11407/.

14. Carrie Saldo, "Two Rockwells Headed to Auction to Fund New Vision for the Berkshire Museum," *Berkshire Eagle*, July 12, 2017, accessed September 18, 2020, https://www.berkshireeagle.com/stories/two-rockwells-headed-to-auction-to-fund-new-vision-for-the-berkshire-museum,513284.

15. Carla Westerman, "The Rebirth of the Delaware Art Museum," *Hunt*, December 15, 2015, accessed September 23, 2020, https://thehuntmagazine.com/feature/the-rebirth-of-the-delaware-art-museum/.

16. "Compliance Report for Financially Motivated Disposal of Items from a Museum Collection," Museums Association, accessed September 14, 2020, https://www.museumsassociation.org/campaigns/ethics/disposal/.

17. Julie Hart (Senior Director, Museum Standards & Excellence, American Alliance of Museums), in discussion with the author, September 14, 2020.

18. "What are Ethics?," American Alliance of Museums, accessed September 1, 2020, http://ww2.aam-us.org/resources/ethics-standards-and-best-practices/ethics.

19. "AAMD Board of Trustees Approves Resolution to Provide Additional Financial Flexibility to Art Museums During Pandemic Crisis," Association of Art Museum Directors, April 15, 2020, https://aamd.org/for-the-media/press-release/aamd-board-of-trustees-approves-resolution-to-provide-additional.

20. Ibid.

21. Joseph Stiglitz, "Inequality, Wealth and Capital," *Queries* 7 (Summer 2015), 57.

22. "'Charitable' Purposes," Internal Revenue Service, accessed September 22, 2020, https://www.irs.gov/charities-non-profits/charitable-purposes.

23. "Community Foundations," Council on Foundations, accessed September 30, 2020, https://www.cof.org/foundation-type/community-foundations-taxonomy.

24. "Equality Act 2010," UK Legislation, accessed September 10, 2020, https://www.legislation.gov.uk/ukpga/2010/15/section/1.

25. Joanna Woronkowicz et al., *Set in Stone: Building America's New Generation of Arts Facilities, 1994–2008* (Chicago: University of Chicago, Cultural Policy Center, 2012).

26. "In Memory of the Corcoran Gallery of Art," Facebook, accessed September 30, 2020, https://www.facebook.com/groups/755880614476949.

27. "Bracelet in the Mingei International Museum Online Collection," Mingei International Museum, accessed September 28, 2020, https://collections.mingei.org/objects-1/info/52615.

28. According to a 2000 study by the Pew Charitable Trusts, the most recent year available, only 10 percent of the house museums studied have an endowment large enough to cover operating costs, 80 percent have more than $1 million in preservation needs, and the average operation budget is $100,000 or less. Jessie Hellmann, "Historic House Museums Facing Struggles," *Gazette*, March 6, 2016.

29. Patrick Sisson, "Rethinking the Modern House Museum," *Curbed*, October 12, 2018, accessed September 30, 2020, https://www.curbed.com/2018/10/12/17967794/museum-home-wright-historic-preservation.

30. "AASLH Statement of Standards and Ethics," American Association for State and Local History, 2018.

31. "AASLH Ethics Position Paper #3: Repurposing of a Historic House/Site," *History News* (Spring 2009).

32. Richard Moe, interview by Brian Lamb, *Q&A*, C-Span, January 18, 2006, https://www.c-span.org/video/?190799-1/qa-richard-moe.

33. "New Historic Real Estate Partnership," National Trust for Historic Preservation, accessed September 30, 2020, https://realestate.savingplaces.org/.

4

Planning for Closure

Planning for closure may seem like a contradiction in terms, since most museums focus all their planning efforts on keeping the doors open. No museum strives to close permanently due to its mandate to hold its assets in perpetual trust for the public, yet we know that it happens to many museums, and not just during recessions and pandemics. Museums have been taught that planning is crucial to success. There is strategic planning, succession planning, disaster preparedness planning, and financial planning in the form of forecasting and modeling. This chapter will guide museums through a healthy and open process to consider all options when faced with an organizational crisis, which will also help in the formulation of a final Plan of Dissolution, should that be the result.

Let's start with a few reasons about why a museum might choose to voluntarily dissolve. Most people assume that museums permanently close because of financial reasons—if they are unable to cover expenses or pay for outstanding debts and likewise also unable to raise enough income. These can be attributed to both external and internal circumstances that are unanticipated— the many crises we are familiar with such as a global pandemic, recession, natural disasters like earthquakes or fires, sudden death of a museum director or major benefactor, discovery of misappropriated funds—or perhaps internal factors that were simply overlooked and not dealt with swiftly enough. In 2010, Federal Reserve Chairman Ben S. Bernanke testified to the Financial Crisis Inquiry Commission in Washington, DC, about what we now call the Great Recession. He stated that, "In discussing the causes of the crisis, it is essential to distinguish between triggers (the particular events or factors that touched off the crisis) and vulnerabilities (the structural weaknesses in the financial system and in regulation and supervision that propagated and amplified the initial shocks)."[1] Either way, proper planning can help to avoid or mitigate risks, or to carefully accept the risks and implement the appropriate policies, procedures, and budgets. Think about who is responsible for assessing risks in your museum. Large companies often have risk managers, certainly museums have Boards of Directors (some with Asset Management Committees), but ultimately it is the entire organization that must be aware of potential risks and the role that each person plays. Yet the key question remains, when do you stop planning to survive and start planning to close? The American Association for State and Local History (AASLH) asks a similar question, "How do you even know if your organization is in trouble or if it is just experiencing a couple of bad years?" They created a two-page list of "Characteristics of Historic House Museums in Peril," to help identify the red flags.[2] If your museum realistically decides that it cannot remedy these problems within a certain time frame, then you need to start planning for closure.

INTENTIONAL CLOSURES

Sometimes, a museum closure may be simply part of the nonprofit natural lifecycle. Dr. Susan Kenny Stevens (2001) describes this as the organization having "neither the purpose, the will, nor the energy to continue."[3] If museums are able to turn around in time, they return to more periods of growth and maturity. However, if this cycle keeps repeating itself, then museums may ultimately weaken so that they are unable to turn around, and then they reach

Nonprofit Lifecycle Stages

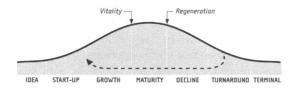

Figure 4.1.   The Nonprofit Lifecycle, 2001. Courtesy of Susan Kenny Stevens

the terminal phase. Public Counsel (2017) proposes additional reasons for voluntary dissolution because of "an assessment that the nonprofit no longer serves its stated mission or constituency, or that its mission or constituency is more than adequately served by other organizations."[4]

CASE IN POINT:

The Clark Center for Japanese Art and Culture, Hanford, California

Born and raised in Hanford in central California, Willard G. "Bill" Clark managed his family ranching and dairy business until he started his own business, World Wide Sires, Ltd., which became the world's largest broker of frozen bull semen for artificial insemination. His interest in Japanese culture started when he was deployed to Japan while serving in the US Navy. In the 1970s he began collecting seriously, and in 1996 he and his wife established the Clark Center for Japanese Art and Culture, advised by Dr. Sherman Lee of the Cleveland Museum of Art. The Center was structured as a 501(c)(3) exempt private foundation, "dedicated to the collection, preservation, exhibition, and study of Japanese arts and culture from the 12th to the 21st century." The Center had a library of 7,000 volumes specializing in Japanese art, a research facility for visiting scholars, an internship program, and it presented lectures and symposia. When Bill and Libby were in their early eighties, they realized they were getting older and that their three adult children were not interested in continuing with the Center. They carefully planned their museum closure, deciding to transfer all assets prior to the dissolution. In 2013 they agreed to donate their art collection to the Minneapolis Institute of Art (MIA), and the bonsai garden to the Shinzen Friendship Garden in nearby Fresno. The agreement stipulated that the current director of the Clark Center would move to the MIA to become its head of the Japanese and Korean Department. It may seem an unlikely move, from rural central California to urban Minneapolis, but Bill and Libby had a personal relationship with Kaywin Feldman, who was the director of the MIA at the time, and the former director of the Fresno Metropolitan Museum of Art and Science back in the mid-1990s. In 2013 Bill Clark commented on the decision,

> I'm a fifth-generation central Californian and I wanted it to be on the West Coast if possible. But when I considered the options, to be honest,

they weren't there. The collection would have "overwhelmed" the University of California at Berkeley and would "just sit in storage" at San Francisco's Asian Art Museum. . . . Minneapolis is one of the great cities in our country. I think it's the perfect home for our collection because they're going to continue our programs.[1]

The MIA agreed to organize two exhibitions a year for the Clark Center for up to five years, and to cover all costs associated with the transfer of the collection (packing, shipping, storage), which they estimated at $200,000 initially and another $200,000 annually. The MIA also acquired additional works from the Clarks' private collection through a $5 million "partial gift, partial purchase" deal. They even remembered their donors, with a message on the Center's website that said, "We are no longer accepting donations and would appreciate it if you would consider making donations to the MIA and/or the Shinzen Garden instead. Also, if you have included the Clark Center in your will as a legacy gift, please consider changing the legacy to the MIA or Shinzen Garden."[2] In 2015, they declared in their Form 990-PF that, "The Clark Center for Japanese Art & Culture has liquidated all its assets and wound up its operations and all remaining funds were paid to the Shinzen Friendship Garden Inc., a 501c3 organization carrying on the mission of the Clark Center." The museum was formally dissolved in June 2015, and Bill Clark died five months later.

NOTES

1. Mary Abbe, "Minneapolis Institute of Arts Given $25 Million Collection of Japanese Art," *Star Tribune*, June 5, 2013, https://www.startribune.com/minneapolis-institute-of-arts-given-25-million-japanese-art-collection/210139451/.
2. "Founder of Clark Center for Japanese Art Dies at 85," *Rafu Shimpo*, December 18, 2015.

Certain nonprofit museums with 501(c)(3) tax exempt status could be considered as private museums,[5] even though they are still incorporated as private nonprofits. What makes them more private in nature is that they are started and funded mostly or entirely by private collectors; the Board of Directors is comprised mainly of family members, business partners, or personal friends; and the museum collection is usually on loan from the founders. These types of museums tend to close because of financial reasons, either because they are for-profit ventures that are no longer making enough profit for their investors, because their founders/funders decide to redirect their investments, or because they did not anticipate the high cost of running a museum. Due to the private nature of how these museums operate, with little transparency and accountability to the public, it is often hard to see early indicators of problems from the outside. For this reason, these types of museums are often described as vanity projects or worse, as tax shelters. In November 2015, Senate Finance Committee Chairman Orrin Hatch (R-Utah) conducted a review of private, nonprofit museums with tax-exempt status, at the request of eleven private foundations questioning if the public interest was being met, and if operations merited the substantial tax benefits afforded to their collector-founders through the tax code. Hatch reported that a number of concerning factors "raise questions about the nature of the relationship between the donor and museum that perhaps merit further scrutiny."[6] There are so many now that there is even an annual Private Museum Conference that started in 2017 in Basel, Switzerland. Two examples of this type of museum are the Marciano Foundation (described in chapter 3) and the Main Museum. Coincidentally, both museums were located in Los Angeles, California, and both closed within a year of each other.

CASE IN POINT:

The Main Museum, Los Angeles, California

The Main Museum (The Main Museum of Los Angeles Art Inc) was a project of Gilmore Associates, part of a real estate development plan for the Historic Core in downtown Los Angeles called Old Bank District 2.0. In 2014, Gilmore Associates (Tom Gilmore and Jerri Perrone, also museum cofounders) announced plans for a 100,000-square-foot "non-museum museum" that would open in 2020. In the meantime, they would operate "Beta Main" out of a smaller space (11,500 square feet) in one of the buildings that opened in 2016. The Main Museum was established as a 501(c)(3) with a small staff and similarly small Board of Directors that consisted of Gilmore, Perrone, and other business partners. Admission was free, there was no permanent collection, and all expenses were covered by Gilmore Associates. Starting around 2018, the museum experienced financial problems due to a decrease in income. Museum executive director Allison Agsten approached the

Pasadena-based ArtCenter College of Design that year to consider a partnership where they could present programming and pay the Main Museum for a presence at its downtown location. By the end of 2018, museum staff suddenly announced that they were leaving, then a couple months later the museum quietly announced that it had closed. The press called it a "mysterious closure" and blogger William Poundstone was quoted as saying, "If there's a moral, maybe it's this: don't start your own museum unless you're prepared to fund it in perpetuity."[1] Then a few months later, the ArtCenter College of Design announced its agreement with Gilmore Associates to rent the Beta Main space for $1 a year for ten years, now called ArtCenter DTLA.[2] Gilmore Associates still retains ownership of the building, but their $55 million museum project never materialized. The museum's 2018 Form 990 includes a Schedule N, indicating the reason for Liquidation, Termination, Dissolution, or Significant Disposition of Assets as "Cancellation of Debt" in the amount of $800,000. The tax return also notes a loss of $1.78 million, of which $1.59 million was designated as depreciation. One can only speculate the details because Gilmore has not given any interviews about the closure and departing staff were asked to sign a nondisclosure agreement.

NOTES

1. Matt Stromberg, "Main Museum's mysterious closure serves as a cautionary tale about funding," *The Art Newspaper*, February 16, 2019, https://www.theartnewspaper.com/news/main-museum-s-mysterious-closure-serves-as-a-cautionary-tale.
2. "ArtCenter Establishes a New Presence in Downtown Los Angeles," May 2, 2019, ArtCenter College of Design, Press Release.

Museums that are created as part of a larger corporate or foundational infrastructure share some of the same vulnerabilities as private museums. A few of these examples include the Wells Fargo History Museums (part of the nonprofit Wells Fargo Foundation of the for-profit Wells Fargo & Company), the National Geographic Museum in Washington, DC (part of the nonprofit National Geographic Society), the Annenberg Space for Photography (part of the nonprofit Annenberg Foundation), and the McCormick Freedom Museum in Chicago, Illinois (completely funded and governed by the nonprofit Robert

R. McCormick Foundation, the second largest stockholder of the for-profit Tribune Company). This type of museum is also more likely to be shut down and often without warning, due to corporate decisions that might occur with leadership changes (CEO and/or board) or from restructuring and refinancing due to shifting priorities and strategies. Because these museums are often housed within larger corporate charitable foundations, it is difficult to examine their museum operations, finances, and leadership structure. These museums may report to the foundation leadership or other departments such as Community Development or Public Relations, which also serve as the museum's major source of funding. During a crisis, the museums might be quickly closed not only to save costs but for the corporation or foundation to focus their resources on what might be perceived as more essential services than running a museum. Two of these museums permanently closed in 2020: Wells Fargo Museums (eleven out of twelve branches closed) and the Annenberg Space for Photography, both cases described in the previous chapter.

Figure 4.2.   McCormick Freedom Tribune Museum, Front Entrance. Photograph by Antonio Vernon, 2007, https://commons.m.wikimedia.org/wiki/File:20070509_McCormick _Tribune_Freedom_Museum.JPG#mw-jump-to-license

CASE IN POINT:

McCormick Freedom Museum, Chicago, Illinois

The museum was named for Colonel Robert R. McCormick (1880–1995), longtime editor and publisher of the *Chicago Tribune* newspaper and a strong supporter of First Amendment rights. In 2005, the museum became incorporated to "enable informed participation in our democracy by demonstrating the relevance of the First Amendment and the role it plays in the ongoing struggle to define and defend freedom." The opening coincided with the fiftieth anniversary of the nonprofit Robert R. McCormick Tribune Foundation that considered the museum as its gift to Chicago. The museum was located on the first two floors of Tribune Tower, a 36-floor neo-Gothic skyscraper on Magnificent Mile in downtown Chicago. All expenses were paid by the Foundation (now called the McCormick Foundation), including very high rent to the Tribune Company that owned the building,[1] and millions of dollars in construction and exhibition design. The museum's Board of Directors was comprised of six executives (current and former) from the *Chicago Tribune*, per Colonel McCormick's will.[2] The museum did not conduct any fundraising or community outreach, and attendance was always low, despite a $5 admission fee that was later waived. The board had anticipated higher attendance numbers, having hired an outside firm to create benchmarks based on the ten or so major cultural institutions around Chicago. It proved challenging to attract downtown visitors and tourists to a "freedom museum," and school visits were difficult because there was no parking for school buses and no designated classroom space.[3] Facing significant debts, the Tribune Company was sold to local investors in 2007 for $8.2 billion, and one year later the company filed for bankruptcy. The following year the museum board decided to close the museum.[4] The museum had also been losing money, with deficits over $1 million each year. The board and staff considered alternative ideas to maintain the programming and staff, and decided to convert operations to a mobile museum that would focus on voter registration efforts in alignment with the Foundation. The exhibitions were stored in various warehouses, but they were mostly interactive, digital exhibitions that soon became outdated. In 2010, the museum name was changed to the McCormick Freedom Project and became absorbed into the Cantigny Foundation of Illinois (also founded by Colonel Robert R.

McCormick), where the mobile unit had been operating out of its parking lot, and the museum filed its Articles of Merger or Consolidation with the Secretary of State in its 2011-990.

NOTES

1. Rent was high because it was market rate for ground-level retail space, using the lobby of the Tribune Company and the second floor of a high-traffic tourist and shopping district.
2. Dave Anderson (former Director, McCormick Freedom Museum), in discussion with the author, September 29, 2020.
3. Nathan Richie (former Director of Exhibits and Programs, McCormick Freedom Museum), in discussion with the author, July 17, 2020.
4. Ibid. Richie stated that, "The Tribune sale was just the catalyst that set off the inevitable."

TEOTWAWKI

How to prepare for The End Of The World As We Know It (TEOTWAWKI)—while this term dates back to the 1960s, predicting the end of the world goes back to at least the first millennium CE, and continues as recently as 2000 and into the new millennium. The fact that all these predictions were wrong has not weaned humanity from its desire to see into the future. In the mid-twentieth century, this desire was channeled into the development of a formal system of futurism. These early futurists realized that it was far more useful to envision and prepare for the many ways that events might play out than to try to make one, fallible prediction. To support this approach, many sectors, including the military, technology, and private energy companies, began to develop sets of scenarios to guide critical decision-making. Scenarios are stories that describe potential futures, used by planners to expand thinking to encompass a variety of plausible or improbable outcomes. For example, the US Army developed scenarios to model the aftermath of nuclear war, and Shell Oil forecast natural, technological, and political factors that would influence the world oil market.

Creating and using scenarios can contribute to the success of organizations in any sector. As the American Planning Association points out, "Scenario planning enables professionals, and the public, to respond dynamically to an unknown future. It assists them with thinking, in advance, about the many ways the future may unfold and how they can be responsive, resilient, and effective, as the future becomes reality."[7] Museums have only recently begun to adopt a formal process for using scenarios in their planning process. The American Alliance of Museums' Center for the Future of Museums (CFM) released the first scenarios developed specifically for museums in 2010. Commissioned by the California Association of Museums, "Tomorrow in the Golden State: Museums and the Future of California" presented five stories of potential futures, together with a framework for using these scenarios in the planning process.[8]

Since that time, the Center for the Future of Museums has continued to help the field identify critical trends, explore potential disruptions, expand their thinking to encompass unexpected futures, and identify steps they can take to create the world they wish to live in. As CFM director Elizabeth Merritt observes, "Exploring scenarios helps you to understand the potential consequences of crucial decisions. Inhabiting potential futures equips museums to create plans that:

- Encompass an appropriate vision for what the organization wants to accomplish,
- Identify appropriate long-term goals,
- Don't rely on vulnerable assumptions,
- Are flexible enough to adapt to changing circumstances and embed appropriate contingencies."[9]

Once you have discussed a few scenarios and created the different narratives—either on your own or assisted by a professional planner with experience in scenarios and forecasting—look at your worst-case scenarios.

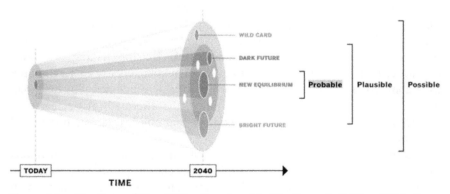

Figure 4.3.   The Cone of Plausibility. *Trendswatch, The Scenario Edition*, 2018. Courtesy of American Alliance of Museums

What steps would you take if you knew that the only other option was to close permanently?

Who would you reach out to for help—your most trusted donors, a community foundation, your public representatives?

What are the early indicators for this crisis?

Think strategically about how to prepare for each scenario, with the goal of keeping the museum alive. Then think strategically about each *closure* alternative and create a plan. What are some closure alternatives? Having considered various scenarios of how the museum's future might play out, create a story that describes your desired future—the best-case outcome—and design a strategy to make that story come true. The rest of this chapter will explore alternatives to closure, along with a few museums that have chosen them, with some resulting in different forms of closure, and others averting closure altogether. A good planning process might save your museum from permanent closure, and if not, it will serve as an important first step to creating your Plan of Dissolution.

MERGERS AND ACQUISITIONS

The difference between a merger and an acquisition is both the process and the result. Mergers happen when two organizations come together to form a new organization, and acquisitions are a takeover of one organization by the other, where the museum that has been taken over has no role in governance. Most museum mergers are actually more like acquisitions.

Museums merge with different types of institutions for several reasons. Probably the most common reason is to identify another institution that can take over operations or assist with expenses. These institutions can be universities, public agencies (the city or county), or other museums or even foundations that are in a solid financial condition. On its website under "Ethics, Standards, and Professional Practices," the American Alliance of Museums confirms that "Some museums have strengthened their operations through mergers."[10] They give examples of many successful mergers: the Perot Museum of Nature and Science, created with the merger of the Dallas Museum of Natural History, The Science Place, and the Dallas Children's Museum; the National Underground Railroad Freedom Center merged with the Cincinnati Museum Center; the Honolulu Academy of Arts and The Contemporary Museum merged to form the Honolulu Museum of Art; the Lancaster Museum of Art and the Demuth Museum merged, maintaining two locations but "one museum with one mission"; and The Museum of the American West (formerly the Gene Autry Western Heritage Museum) in Los Angeles merged with the Women of the West Museum in 2002, and with the Southwest Museum in 2003, to become the Autry National Center (later renamed the Autry Museum of the American West).

Ideally these mergers are planned out well in advance of a crisis and are mutually beneficial to both parties, but often mergers become the last resort before permanent closure or even after a museum has decided to dissolve. The problem with the latter case is that when faced with no other choice, the museum is not in a strong position to negotiate the terms of the merger or the acquisition, which brings us back to the importance of planning early and choosing carefully. Mergers and acquisitions are meant as alternatives to permanent closure, which can still happen if partnerships fail.

First review your Articles of Incorporation, Bylaws, and your museum history to determine any restrictions on transferring assets and original intentions by museum founders. One of the most famous examples of original intent is the Barnes Foundation, which was restricted by its founder, Alfred C. Barnes, from moving, selling, or lending any paintings, allowing only 60,000 visitors each year to its 1925 buildings in the suburbs, and prohibiting color reproductions. Losing money and visitors, the Foundation wanted to move from Merion, Pennsylvania, to downtown Philadelphia. After a lengthy court battle, extensive media coverage and public protest, the courts overruled the trust and allowed the move in 2012. On its website, the museum defended its move as "to better serve Dr. Barnes's educational mission." If there are restrictions for your museum, carefully discuss not only the instructions but their meanings and any supporting documentation, in order to completely understand them both within the context of different times and circumstances.

Next review all your current partners, including programmatic partners, local community partners, institutions that may be represented on your Board of Directors or Advisory Boards, and neighboring organizations. Do not limit yourself to just local partners but think nationally like the Clark Center for Japanese Art and Culture. As you gather with staff and board members, ask yourselves, who would you want to partner with, and why? Think out of the box, think about your mission in a very broad way, and think about your museum community. Who else shares your same values? Who else could benefit from a partnership with you?

Make a list of your tangible and intangible assets and liabilities and prioritize what aspects of your museum are the most important to preserve and why, and which can be modified or even discarded.

> Are there debts that need to be paid off, will staff be guaranteed to keep their jobs, what percentage of board membership will each organization have?
> How will the collection be integrated into the partnering institution?

Will you stipulate how the collection will be stored, exhibited, and credited?

Will your donors continue to be acknowledged if, perhaps, they have named a staff position, a physical space, or even a program that will be transferred as well?

These are just some of the questions that need to be answered, ideally well before you start looking for partners.

CASE IN POINT:

USC Pacific Asia Museum, Pasadena, California

When the University of Southern California (USC) partnered with the Pacific Asia Museum in 2013 (founded in 1971), I was hired as interim deputy director to handle the transition together with the director of the university campus museum. The Pacific Asia Museum had serious financial troubles, the previous executive director had just left after two years, and a board member was serving as interim executive director. They had already acquired an auction estimate to sell the best of the approximately 15,000-piece Asian art collection. Another board member's husband found himself at an event with the president of USC and casually suggested that they take over the museum. The president took him seriously and proceeded to conduct a thorough analysis of the museum. The university agreed to assume the museum's debts and also all its assets, including its collection and building, a replica of a Chinese imperial palace built in 1926 in the National Register of Historic Places, centrally located in downtown Pasadena with a large parking lot. The museum's name became USC Pacific Asia Museum, and everything was immediately rebranded. All museum staff were given six-month contracts and evaluated to determine if they would be hired as permanent staff again, or if their contract would not be renewed. Numerous museums operations were taken over by university departments such as Human Resources, IT, Facilities, Communications, Rentals, and Development, the museum's library was folded into the university library, and a master plan was created to handle building improvements. The former museum board members had a few seats on the Transition Team, which lasted around six months, but in reality the new governing body of the museum was the USC Board of Trustees because the museum now operated under the university's educational 501(c)(3). The university initially gave the museum three years to become completely financially self-sufficient, which was unrealistic and never happened, given all the unforeseen challenges with the transition. Fundraising was more complicated, going through university bureaucracy, competing with other university grants and funding needs, and trying to retain the old donors while courting new ones. The community of Pasadena was wary of the new university management, and many donors, docents, and volunteers were very upset with the changes, but many also stayed and even new ones joined. The museum's history, name, collections, programs, and building all stayed intact. Some say that the new museum looks more like a professional museum now, while others say that it has lost its charm and uniqueness. Many have asked me why the university would want to take over this museum, located fourteen miles away from campus where they already have another art museum (USC Fisher Museum of Art). The university was very focused on Asia and the Pacific Rim, as well as attracting students from Asia and Chinese billionaire investors in Los Angeles, and it has six international offices in Asia. "This is a natural connection for us," said former USC Vice Provost Robert Cooper. "It's an extension of what we're already doing as a Pacific Rim university with many interests in Asia. It's wonderful on both sides, because it provides stability for the museum for the future, and gives USC something it didn't have before."[1]

NOTE

1. Mike Boehm, "USC Absorbs Pasadena's Pacific Asia Museum in Friendly Takeover," *Los Angeles Times*, November 19, 2013, accessed September 12, 2020, http://www.ucira.ucsb.edu/usc-absorbs-pasadenas-pacific-asia-museum-in-friendly-takeover/.

Mergers and acquisitions do not always require a dissolution; it depends on the terms of the agreement. For example, when the Textile Museum merged with George Washington University in 2015 (both located in Washington, DC), the Textile Museum retained its name, logo, 501(c)(3) status, and its collection that is on permanent loan to the university. Aside from the collection, the museum's other major asset was a large mansion from 1908 on Embassy Row. The museum wanted to sell the building because of growing maintenance costs,[11] and the need for more storage. As a condition of the merger, the museum sold its buildings, with the proceeds contributing over

Figure 4.4. Joint logo from GWU website, https://museum.gwu.edu/

$17 million to a "TM@GW" endowment to cover ongoing costs of staffing, exhibitions, programs, and collections care. The Textile Museum is now responsible for raising funding for textile programs and exhibitions, and George Washington University pays for facilities, custodial, electric, provides central services (legal, financial, human resources), and has fiduciary control.

Once you have found a partner, hire an attorney to help with the negotiations, and think of this as a business deal. You have been entrusted to care for your collection and your museum as a public benefit, and it is your responsibility to ensure that the public will *continue* to benefit from this merger or acquisition. If you cannot do this, then the courts may intervene (voluntarily or involuntarily) and decide in favor of how they view the public benefit. Consider what is best for your museum, for your collection, and for your community. How will your museum and local communities react to this change, how should they be involved in the discussions (planning before and with your new partner), and how should you break the news? There will be surprise, anger, and even opposition, so be ready with a good communications plan (and even a public relations agency if possible).

CASE IN POINT:

Newport Harbor Art Museum and Laguna Art Museum, Orange County, California

In 1962, thirteen women rented space in the Balboa Pavilion to exhibit modern and contemporary art, and six years later this became the Newport Harbor Art Museum. The museum moved twice after that, in 1972 and 1977, and in the 1980s their big plan to build a new ten-acre site with the Irvine Co. and architect Renzo Piano fell apart. Nearby there was an important artist colony in Laguna Beach from the early 1900s, and in 1918 the Laguna Beach Art Association was founded with an exhibition space. That original space went through numerous

renovations and expansions and, in 1972, it became known as the Laguna Beach Museum of Art, and then in 1986 the Laguna Art Museum
(LAM). These two museums, Newport Harbor Art Museum and LAM,
had similar missions and were in close proximity. In 1980, prompted by
a national recession and to avoid insolvency, the museums began discussing the idea of a merger, agreeing that consolidating their resources
and collections into a new and bigger museum would cut administrative
costs and facilitate fundraising that was difficult because of competition in the small funding community. The intention, as specified in
LAM's fifteen-year strategic plan, was to combine the two museums
and dissolve LAM in order to establish the new museum, to be called
the Orange County Museum of Art (OCMA).[1] The OCMA would adopt
the LAM's Bylaws and nonprofit status. Staff was to be consolidated
with a possible reduction, the new director would be the LAM director,
and the location would be Newport Harbor Art Museum's space near
Fashion Island. While there was no agreement on keeping the Laguna
museum site (partly because the location was limited), there were discussions about keeping both sites if there was enough funding. Because
the Newport museum focused on post-war California art and LAM focused on historical and contemporary California art, the opportunity to
combine the collections would be "a unique and invaluable resource for
the entire community." The Newport museum chose as its negotiator a
trustee who was general partner of a venture capital firm. The LAM also
chose a trustee who was a private investor with experience in corporate
mergers.[2] Both museums had combined debts of $377,000 that had to be
resolved before a merger occurred. The problem was that the LAM was
a membership organization, so a majority of the 1,500 general members
had to ratify the 26–0 vote already taken by both boards to approve the
merger. Two groups of longtime members soon formed—Save Laguna
Art Museum (SLAM) and Motivated Museum Members—and sued the
museum to stop the merger. "A merger means they will have ripped
the heart out of our city," they cried.[3] The groups wanted to keep the
historic Laguna museum building open, but still operating under the
new museum. The terms of a compromise agreement created a new
nonprofit 501(c)(3) corporation named LAM Heritage Corporation that
took ownership of the Laguna museum building, committed to raise
two-thirds of the former LAM's annual budget, and soon changed its
name to the Laguna Art Museum. It also acquired part ownership of
the collection and endowment, while the rest (mostly contemporary art)

stayed with the new Orange County Museum of Art. In the end, it was the Laguna Beach community that stopped the process of permanently closing the LAM. They didn't want change and were very protective of their seventy-five-year-old museum. Today, LAM operates independently and has had most of its art "gifted back" by OCMA,[4] along with half of its original endowment and ownership of its land and building on Laguna's idyllic Cliff Drive.

NOTES

1. Bolton Colburn (former Director of the Laguna Art Museum) and Susan M. Anderson (former Chief Curator of the Laguna Art Museum), in discussion with the author, September 11, 2020.
2. Cathy Curtis and Zan Dubin, "Talks Resume for Merger of O.C. Museums, *Los Angeles Times*, February 2, 1996.
3. Zan Dubin and Michael G. Wagner, "Boards Vote to Join OC Museums," *Los Angeles Times*, February 28, 1996.
4. In 2009, the Orange County Museum of Art "quietly sold 18 pieces of California Impressionist paintings to a Laguna Beach collector, whose name is not being made public." The sale resulted in less than $1 million, which former LAM director Bolton Colburn called "a bargain." These paintings were originally owned by the Laguna Art Museum, then ownership transferred to the OCMA with the merger. The LAM was not notified about the sale or given an opportunity to purchase the works, much like a previous sale in 1996, and the Laguna arts community remains bitter. Barbara Diamond, "Our Laguna: Art Museum Merger Attempt Still Stings," *Los Angeles Times*, June 19, 2009.

A final point about mergers and acquisitions relates to public museums, meaning those that are governed (fully or partially) by governmental agencies: city, county, state, and federal government. During times of crisis, museums often wish they could be rescued by their city or county, envisioning a more secure source of income and protection, yet public museums are just as susceptible as any other. Chapter 3 discussed how the Detroit Institute of Arts was threatened by the City of Detroit which sought to sell the museum's collections when it declared bankruptcy.

At the state level, the Illinois State Museum in Springfield was closed for nine months in 2015 by Illinois Governor Bruce Rauner when there was a budget stalemate regarding a debt of $4 billion. In an attempt to cut $400 million across the state, the Department of Natural Resources that manages the museum proposed that the museum's budget decrease from $6.3 to $1.5 million, retaining only four staff for security and maintenance out of sixty-eight total before the closure. Museum staff had decided to unionize only eleven months earlier, and the union filed a lawsuit to stop the layoffs.[12] The governor's decision was not supported by many public officials, museum supporters in the community, and other state museums. A public hearing by the Commission on Government Forecasting and Accountability ruled against the governor's decision, but their decision was nonbinding.[13] When the museum reopened, it took time to increase the staff and bring back visitors. Many staff had retired or moved on, and others not part of the union were laid off. The museum had five facilities around the state before the closure: two closed permanently, and four reopened. After a very bumpy road, now with a new director, a new governor, and a $4 million budget, the museum "feels very secure."[14]

The federal government shut down for thirty-five days between December 22, 2018, and January 25, 2019 (the longest in US history), because Congress and the White House could not agree on the spending bill. Nineteen museums are part of the Smithsonian Institution, largely funded by the federal government. These museums started to close on January 2, losing millions of dollars in revenue, and 350,000 federal employees were placed on furlough. A previous government shutdown, in May 2013, lasted sixteen days because of mandatory budget cuts ("supercommittee sequestration cuts") that required the Smithsonian to cut 5.2 percent of its budget or $42 million. There were random exhibition closures at six museums in DC, and they estimate losing $4 million in revenue. The American Alliance of Museums wrote a "Shutdown Prevention and Economic Impact Issue Brief" (2019) as part of its advocacy efforts with the federal government. However, even without total government shutdowns, each year the Smithsonian Board of Regents, along with other advocacy groups such as the AAM, work closely with legislators on all levels and from all political parties to not only maintain federal funding of the Smithsonian Institute and the Institute of Museum and Library Services, but to increase funding. They have consistently been successful.[15]

CASES IN POINT:

Museum of Ventura County, California

The Ventura Pioneer Society was founded in 1892 and became the Museum of Ventura County, opened in 1913, and was incorporated as a private nonprofit 501(c)(3) in 1957, fully funded by the County of

Ventura. Everything was going fine until Proposition 13 was passed by the California legislature in 1978, cutting property taxes and substantially reducing income for state and local governments. In response, Ventura County cut all its funding to the museum. A passionate museum supporter came forward, donating not only her own money but actively fundraising within the community and covering as much as 75 percent of all museum expenses. That saved the museum, but then the donor died in 2000 and the museum experienced more tough times. A $10 million capital campaign targeted for 2008 was cut short by the recession. Ventura County had been fundraising for its new Agriculture Museum, which opened in 2011 as a satellite of the Museum of Ventura County. Fundraising was so successful for the Agriculture Museum that a reserve fund was created. In desperation, the museum started borrowing from this fund until it was depleted in 2016, while at the same time increasing its budget from $1.9 to $2.2 million. After careful planning and tough discussions, the museum realized that it had only two options left: close permanently or be rescued by the County government. First, they knew that they had to prove themselves again to the County, so the entire Board of Directors resigned. In six months, they raised $1.7 million from the City and County to start an endowment. But that wasn't enough. After the devastating wildfires hit Ventura in December 2017, they turned their focus to becoming more of a community center and were able to receive $2.25 million in total from the County for the next five years. Executive director Elena Brokaw admits that the key to their success was asking for help and being honest, "People were afraid to acknowledge how bad things were."[1] The museum continues to thrive today with the support of the County government and the community of Ventura.

Pacific Grove Museum of Natural History, California

Since 1883, the Pacific Grove Museum of Natural History has been owned by the City of Pacific Grove on the central coast of California. During the 2008 recession, the museum was sorely neglected and budget cuts over the years led to a volunteer-run museum with only one employee. On the verge of permanently closing, a group of community supporters stepped in and decided to create an independent nonprofit foundation. The museum was incorporated in 1967 as a 501(c)(3) as the Pacific Grove Museum of Natural History Association, but this was dissolved in 2010 following the creation of the Museum Foundation of Pacific Grove Inc. in 2009. Under this new arrangement, the City owns the building and collections, and the Museum Foundation agreed to "operate, maintain, advance, and enhance" the museum. Ten years later, the museum is thriving with thirteen full-time employees and a $1 million endowment. They serve over 50,000 visitors a year, many of them from the underserved areas, and have embarked on a new capital campaign to raise $2.1 million for renovations. Executive director Jeanette Kihs confirms the importance of negotiating well as central to their success. Originally, the museum received sliding payments from the City with a fixed amount, then the museum's attorney convinced them to modify the arrangement to a percentage basis so that as the City becomes stronger, so does the museum. Reflecting on this journey in the midst of a pandemic, Kihs says that "We're getting comfortable with being uncomfortable about the unknown future."[2]

NOTES

1. Susana Bautista, Elena Brokaw, and Jeannette Kihs, "Museums on the Edge: Stories of Transformation and Failure," online presentation at the California Association of Museums Lunch & Learn, March 6, 2020, https://www.youtube.com/watch?v=WhWF59i3rrA&t=3s.
2. Ibid.

SCALE DOWN

If the problem is financial, the only real solutions are to increase revenue and decrease expenses. First let's focus on the latter. There are many ways to cut expenses, and they are all difficult decisions to make. Some options are to cancel or postpone planned exhibitions; eliminate certain programs; close facilities; cut out professional development in the budget such as attending conferences, subscriptions, and memberships; institute a hiring freeze, a salary increase freeze, and a halt on temporary labor; make cuts in salary or reduce hours; and certainly the most difficult of all is to reduce staff through layoffs or furloughs. These decisions are made by senior management and Boards of Directors (ideally working together) based on legal and contractual constraints, organizational priorities, mission, and values.

On the other side of the spectrum, there has been an astonishing expansion of museums over the last three decades, opening new satellites around town to become more integrated into their communities, around the country, or even around the world in some cases (the Louvre Museum, the Guggenheim Museum). Museums have built more classrooms as they prioritize education, they have had to accommodate growing collections, and they have torn down old buildings as maintenance costs become unwieldy. An important study called *Set in Stone* (University of Chicago, 2012) researched cultural infrastructure building projects in the United States between 1994 and 2008. During this period, museums spent nearly $6 billion on new building projects that peaked in 2002, with almost half going over budget.[16] The results for most were higher operating costs and lower-than-expected attendance.[17] In 2016, *Art Newspaper* conducted a survey of 500 museums, revealing that 10 percent had undergone an expansion between 2007 and 2014. Out of these museums, annual attendance increased an average of 14.1 percent, compared with 10.2 percent for museums that did not expand.[18]

Interestingly, the Great Recession did not stop museums from expanding; they simply made adjustments. The Nelson-Atkins Museum of Art in Kansas City, Missouri, had just opened its new Bloch Building in 2007, so in response to the recession it cut hours and turned down its thermostat. In 2008, the Los Angeles County Museum of Art refinanced $383 million of adjustable-rate bonds it issued to pay for a major building renovation. In addition to programming cuts, it established a hiring freeze on all nonrevenue-raising positions.[19] *Set in Stone* also reports the unfortunate cuts and elimination of education programs and expensive special exhibitions to focus on permanent collections.[20] Sometimes building projects were just put on hold, or canceled completely, as reported in 2010 by Martha Morris, Associate Professor Emerita of Museum Studies, George Washington University.[21]

During other times of financial crisis, however, museums decide to reduce their physical footprint. In response to COVID-19, the three museums below scaled down their physical spaces during the month of June 2020. Since a peak in 2016, major museum building projects around the world have been slowly declining, according to AEA Consulting's annual Cultural Infrastructure Index. The decrease will certainly continue after 2020, as physical spaces are being adapted to accommodate social distancing or for entirely new uses.[22]

CASE IN POINT:

The Metropolitan Museum of Art:
The Breuer, New York City, New York

In 2015, the Metropolitan Museum of Art (Met) rented the Whitney Museum's former Madison Avenue building ten blocks away, but discussions started as early as 2011. The Met Breuer satellite space opened in March 2016, focusing on modern and contemporary art, after spending $13 million in renovations. The contract was to last from 2016–2023, at $17 million a year rent. In 2018, however, the Met announced that it would leave the space in 2020 and sublet the building to the Frick Collection, which was looking for a space during their renovation and expansion five blocks away. Although the Met had serious financial troubles in 2016 and 2017 with a $15 million operating deficit,[1] Daniel H. Weiss, the Met's president and chief executive, declared that "We didn't start chasing the possibility of getting out of the lease early . . . maybe there's a way [the Frick] would benefit from the building, as we're thinking about moving in a different direction."[2] The Whitney's director confirmed that the Met's lease has a sublet clause, stating, "as long as you take care of it and do everything you're supposed to do, it's fine."[3] The Met still retains its second satellite space, the Met Cloisters, just six miles north.

NOTES

1. "We've had financial challenges—significant ones—over the last couple of years that have culminated over the past year," said Weiss, "and a rather significant need to reorganize the institution and to retrench our finances." "NYC's Met Working Through Financial Difficulties," *Philanthropy News Digest*, May 17, 2017, accessed September 10, 2020, https://philanthropynews digest.org/news/nyc-s-met-working-through-financial-difficulties.

2. Victoria Stapley-Brown, Nancy Kenney, and Helen Stoilas, "Met Plans to Leave Breuer Building Making Way for the Frick," *Art Newspaper*, September 21, 2018, accessed September 10, 2020, https://www.theartnewspaper.com/news/met-to-leave-breuer-building-making-way-for-the-frick.

3. Ibid.

CASE IN POINT:

Children's Museum of Richmond, Virginia

In 1981, the Children's Museum opened in a small 8,100-square-foot building. It then moved to a new 44,000-square-foot building in downtown Richmond in 2000. Intent on serving children and families closer to where they work and live, they branched out: the Children's Museum Short Pump opened in 2010 in the West End, a location in Chesterfield opened in 2012, and one in Fredericksburg's Eagle Village Shopping Center opened in 2014. All four branches were very successful, but the museum was heavily dependent (70%) on earned revenue from admissions, birthday parties, and field trips. Having closed temporarily since March 14 due to COVID-19 restrictions, the museum laid off and furloughed forty-two staff across all locations. Virginia allowed for museums to reopen mid-June at reduced capacity, but they wouldn't be able to use any interactive exhibitions. Then in June, the museum closed its Fredericksburg branch and, shortly after that, also the Short Pump branch. The museum only owned its Richmond building and was paying market-rate rent at the other three locations, which amounted to around 25 percent of the budgets. The Fredericksburg branch alone had annual operating expenses of $350,000. The museum's president and CEO, Danielle Ripperton, admitted that, "If we kept all the locations, that means the organization would not survive."[1] Having in place a Location Committee on the board helped the museum to quickly evaluate all the leases and agreements to make the difficult decision together with senior staff. They recognized that they needed to protect the Richmond building, and this was all they could do to ensure viability. We're a children's museum, said Ripperton, "we don't have a Picasso to sell."[2] The museum relocated exhibitions to the remaining branches, and reopened to their members on September 12, 2020, with reduced days and timed tickets. Ripperton acknowledges that the public was disappointed with the closures, but they were open and transparent with their community and had a communications strategy from the beginning.

NOTES

1. Neda Ulaby, "So Much For 'Please Touch,' After COVID-19, Kids' Museums Will Be Less Hands-On," *Morning Edition*, National Public Radio,

July 1, 2020, https://www.npr.org/2020/07/01/881626432/so-much-for-please -touch-after-covid-19-kids-museums-will-be-less-hands-on.

2. Danielle Ripperton (President and CEO, Children's Museum of Richmond), in discussion with the author, October 19, 2020.

CASE IN POINT:

A+D Museum, Los Angeles, California

The Architecture + Design Museum (A+D) opened in 2001 in a donated space in the historic Bradbury Building in downtown Los Angeles. When that building was sold in 2003, the museum moved to a temporary location in West Hollywood. In 2006 they found a permanent home on Wilshire Boulevard on Museum Row, across the street from the Los Angeles County Museum of Art. Four years later, they moved to a new building a block away. Forced to move once again in 2015 because of the new Metro Line, the museum returned to downtown, this time in a warehouse in the trendy Arts District. When the pandemic hit, they used the crisis as an opportunity to reimagine the museum in light of a changing society. In June 2020, the Board of Directors decided to close their physical building and instead operate with a "network format." As the museum's website states (aplusd.org), "The pandemic pushed us to question how a museum transcends its physical boundaries, continues to evolve as an institution with societal needs. The shift to a hybrid model comes as a natural progression of the museum's history as an itinerant space." The museum already had a Beyond Walls Strategic Planning Committee in place well before the pandemic, which discussed how to meet its mission and serve a "wider, increasingly inclusive audience" beyond the limitations of a physical building. Executive director Anthony Morey describes the museum's core values as "being nimble and responsive to current events, being experimental." "We hope to make the city our building, he adds. The building isn't the crown jewel, the exhibits are."[1] The best part is that the museum was able to retain all of its staff because, along with the building closure, they also conducted an institutional restructuring that added a new position of digital researcher.

NOTE

1. Antonio Pacheco, "LA's A+D Museum to Close Physical Location and Go Virtual," *Archinect*, June 18, 2020, accessed September 10, 2020, https:// archinect.com/news/article/150203111/la-s-a-d-museum-to-close-physical -location-and-go-virtual.

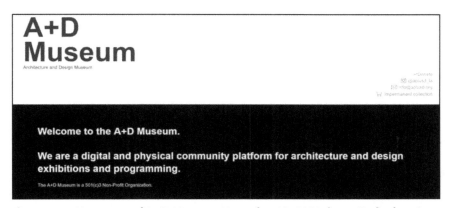

A+D
Museum
Architecture and Design Museum

Welcome to the A+D Museum.

We are a digital and physical community platform for architecture and design exhibitions and programming.

The A+D Museum is a 501(c)3 Non-Profit Organization

Figure 4.5.   Homepage of A+D Museum. November 10, 2020, https://aplusd.org/

MORE MONEY

In order to increase revenue during a crisis, there are several options that museums consider. Museums that are in a better financial situation already have cash reserves and a bank line of credit, which can be renegotiated to increase the borrowing limit. They also have assets such as property that can be sold, collections that should not be sold for operating expenses, and an endowment(s) that may be restricted and whose principal should never be touched (both discussed previously). If museums have received restricted grants for programs, exhibitions, or special initiatives, they can approach funders with a request to reallocate part or all grant monies to pay for general operating expenses and/or staff salaries. Funders are more open to allowing these requests when there is a widespread crisis affecting museums such as a pandemic or a natural disaster.

One more option that is usually not discussed in the context of financial crises is the *Crisis Appeal*, also known as an Emergency Appeal or a Rapid Response Appeal. Private foundations and government agencies often act quickly to provide museums with emergency funds. During the pandemic, the J. Paul Getty Trust created a $10 million LA Arts COVID-19 Relief Fund to support Los Angeles–based nonprofit museums and visual arts organizations, and the California Arts Council created a California Relief Fund for Artists and Cultural Practitioners, using $920,000 from its general fund, and the federal government passed the CARES Act (Coronavirus Aid, Relief and Economic Security Act) with its $150 billion Coronavirus Relief Fund. But often these funds are not enough, or some museums may not qualify, so they launch their own *Emergency Appeal*. Museums usually have strong opinions about this; they either love the idea or they hate it. Those that love it talk about the success of crowdfunding platforms such as GoFundMe and social media appeals that reach a wide community base that tends to be younger. Those on the other side prefer to keep their crises to themselves and show a positive and strong public face, or may prefer other means of fundraising. Whatever you believe, we do know that after museums permanently close, it is not surprising to hear from community and museum members that they had no idea the museum was in such dire straits. People are quoted in the news as showing their disappointment and regret that they could not do more to help. So, if you are in trouble and need emergency help, who do you ask, and how?

The museum should already have a strong relationship with its funding community, including local foundations and major donors, as well as individual members and supporters. Crafting the right message is important. Some questions to resolve beforehand are: who delivers the message, how should it align with your organizational culture (i.e., serious, lighthearted, arts or community focused), and which platforms should be used (social media, email, printed mailings)? Timing is the hardest part; launch too soon and it's not enough of a crisis, launch too late and it's too big of a risk if you don't raise the money. Here are some great examples of museums that were saved just in time, some by incredible luck, and others by a well-organized campaign.

CASE IN POINT:

The Military Museum of Fort Worth, Texas

In 2017, the Military Museum of Fort Worth announced that it was closing its doors on March 11, due to a drop in attendance and lack of funding. With free admission, the museum relied on donations for 40 percent of its budget, and the Organization for Texas Military Education for the rest, for a total of $17,500 in annual expenses. The museum had about 3,000 visitors a year—85 percent from out of town or state—which for some reason decreased to 1,000. The closure announcement ran in the local newspaper on March 2, 2017, where the executive director Tyler Alberts talked about using the collection as a "mobile museum" to set up displays around town, and that he hoped another military museum would open again. "If someone decides to take that on, we'd be more than happy to join in," he added.[1] And then a miracle happened. One day before they planned to close, they heard from another local military organization named Roll Call that committed to fund the museum for six months. Roll Call is an all-volunteer nonprofit dedicated to honoring and serving local veterans since 2014. The two organizations created a partnership and used those six months to find ways to grow the museum, increase attendance, and identify a better and bigger location. Today the museum is still in existence and is now part of the Fort Worth Stockyards National Historic District.[2]

NOTES

1. Domingo Ramirez Jr., "That Little Fort Worth Military Museum is Closing its Doors," *Fort Worth Star-Telegram*, March 2, 2017, accessed September 10, 2020, https://www.star-telegram.com/news/local/fort-worth/article136025408.html.

2. Fort Worth Stockyards National Historic District, Fort Worth, Texas, accessed November 24, 2020, https://www.fortworthstockyards.org/play/military-museum-fort-worth.

CASE IN POINT:

The US Space & Rocket Center, Huntsville, Alabama

With the vision of Dr. Wernher von Braun and land donated by the US Army, the US Space & Rocket Center opened in 1970. The museum receives over 650,000 visitors each year, is the Official Visitor Center for NASA's Marshall Space Flight Center, has one of the largest collections of rockets and space memorabilia in the world, and is the state's top paid tourist attraction. Due to COVID-19, the museum lost 66 percent of its annual revenue or $28 million, and it laid off one-third of its full-time staff and 700 part-time workers, and furloughed the rest.[1] Because they are operated by the state of Alabama, they are not eligible for state or federal COVID relief funds. In July 2020, they launched an "emergency fundraising effort" that focused just on saving their very popular Space Camp. The chairman of the Alabama Space Science Exhibit Commission declared at a news conference, "We are now struggling for our very survival."[2] There were newspaper articles, social media (Facebook and Twitter with the hashtag #SaveSpaceCamp), television (CNN and WXII 12 News), and a GoFundMe campaign which stated:

> At this time, we have exhausted all funding possibilities, and without your support the US Space & Rocket Center and Space Camp will have to close in October. However, we firmly believe that failure is not an option, so we are turning to you. We need the support of our fellow science enthusiasts, Space Camp alumni and anyone who believes in the spirit of exploration to help all systems return to go. Will you chip in today and help us raise $1.5 million? This will support us through the winter and allow us time to plan for a future filled with Space Camp and scientific discovery. We have to save Space Camp, and we know that together we can reach mission accomplished.

The result of this emergency campaign was that, in just ten days, the museum raised $1,561,027, more than its $1.5 million goal. The money was raised from 8,281 people across fifty states and in thirty-six countries including Alabama football coach Nick Saban and his wife Terry, a $250,000 donation from technology company SAIC, and a $500,000 contribution from the Boeing Company. Four months after the GoFundMe page was created, the museum continues to raise money, as a successful grassroots campaign, bolstered by a few major donors.

NOTES

1. "'Save Space Camp' Drive Pulls in More than $1 Million in Days after Pandemic Losses Threaten Closure," WXII 12 News, Associated Press, August 4, 2020, accessed August 5, 2020, https://www.wxii12.com/article/save-space-camp-drive-pulls-in-more-than-dollar1-million-in-days-after-covid-losses-threaten-closure/33515101#.
2. Ibid.

Figure 4.6. Go Fund Me campaign for the U.S. Space & Rocket Center. November 27, 2020

Sometimes, museum leaders can use the crisis threat of permanent closure as a means to raise money and draw attention to a museum, regardless of its financial situation. This tactic is very risky and causes undue stress for everyone involved in the museum. This happened with the John & Mable Ringling Museum of Art, years after it had transferred to the University of Florida, under new university leadership. Former museum director Dr. John Wetenhall describes this case in his own words, highlighting the need for binding agreements to ensure that planning and hard work are not for naught.[23]

CASE IN POINT:

The John & Mable Ringling Museum of Art, Sarasota, Florida

I remember my first museum merger almost entirely by the people who made it happen. Two members of the museum board realized that moving the official "State Museum" from Florida's Department of State to a university could provide new funding streams for the desperately struggling, decaying museum. The president of Florida State University, a magnificent visionary named Sandy D'Alemberte, recognized the academic value and public prestige that a museum could offer his university, notwithstanding its distant campus 300 miles away. As a condition of the merger, he secured legislative appropriations to renovate the original 1920s art museum and install security systems and climate controls, as well as funding to restore a majestic theater interior imported from Asolo, Italy, and to complete renovation of the once-stately Ringling Mansion, the "Ca d'Zan." A super-connected community volunteer who chaired the museum board worked tirelessly to earn community support, meeting by meeting, luncheon speech by luncheon speech. Her successor brokered a deal with Governor Jeb Bush to release funding for a visitor center, a new circus museum, and desperately required improvements across the sixty-acre landscaped estate. My predecessor, acting director Arland Christ-Janer, had come out of retirement as a college president to rebuild staff morale and engage community support. I spent nine years overseeing the restoration and expansion, empowering a professional staff, and doing my best to transform the once-forgotten cultural jewel into a must-see tourist destination and a respected participant in the national and international community of museums. We—leaders, professionals, volunteers, and supporters—together implemented $100 million in physical improvements and secured over $50 million for operating endowment to return the Ringling Estate to its original splendor and assure its future for generations to come. Over time, though, mergers are less about individuals than institutions. The charismatic visionaries, dealmakers, and passionate worker-bees eventually drift away. What remains is what matters. I learned this during the mortgage crisis of 2008–2009, when I read in the local Sarasota newspaper that our museum was about to be closed and the entire staff laid off, with no one but a security officer at the gate to turn visitors away. The threat was merely brinksmanship by a new university president seeking to preserve legislative funding. The closure never happened, but university administrators who had nothing to do with the merger reappropriated the original funding streams that the museum had brought to the university. It was shortly thereafter that my title changed to "former director," as I learned through crisis a hard truth about mergers: the spoken promises, understandings, and assurances of individuals—regardless of authority, integrity, or handshake commitments—are not binding on their successors. The vision, character, and trust of the people who had grounded our merger in success became our weakness in their absence. When it comes to long-term obligations and core financial commitments, you have to write them down.

COLLECTIONS STEWARDSHIP

One of the most critical parts of the planning process—whether it is scenario planning, general strategic planning, or crafting a Plan of Dissolution—is how to deal with museum collections. There are legal requirements for the distribution of assets and also ethical considerations, as were discussed previously, which are specific to nonprofit, private, and publicly owned collections. In times of crisis and change, museums may consider alternative possibilities for their collection, such as transfer to a charitable trust as in the case of the Detroit Institute of Arts that protected it from the City of Detroit, transfer to another institution or museum for either short-term care (as in the case below) or long-term ownership, return to the donor(s), or sale (private or auction) to use the proceeds to pay for debts or care for the rest of the collection. You must consider all possibilities and each of their consequences to the museum, the public, and the donors. Julia Pagel, secretary general of the Network of European Museum Organisations, reminds us that, "A museum isn't just a repository of individual items. The works speak to each other in their context. If you tear that apart and sell it, for example, how do you get that context and that history back?"[24]

CASE IN POINT:

The Civil War Museum of Philadelphia, Pennsylvania

As the oldest chartered Civil War institution in the country since 1888, the Civil War Museum of Philadelphia was founded by the Military Order of the Loyal Legion of the United States. Problems started in 2000, when the museum was housed in a mansion with shrinking donations and attendance. The museum wanted to move to Richmond, Virginia, the former capital of the Confederacy, but the Pennsylvania Attorney General's Office intervened and blocked the move. In 2008 the museum tried and failed to sell the mansion and move into a historic bank building in Independence Park. In search of a new home in Philadelphia, the museum put its entire collection in boxes and placed it for safekeeping with the Gettysburg Foundation, partially exhibited at the Gettysburg Battlefield Museum and Visitors Center. Then in 2016, they came to a decision. As stated on their website (civilwarmuseumphila.org),

> After much consideration of changed circumstances in the region's philanthropic environment, the Board of Governors determined that it needed to seek a new strategy that could ensure that the collection would be preserved and kept intact in perpetuity, be cared for at the highest standards, and be accessible to the public. Rather than continuing to pursue the goal

of building a new museum, a plan was developed to transfer the collection to the Gettysburg Foundation where it will be part of the extraordinary collection in the Gettysburg Museum and Visitors Center and in the iconic setting of the Gettysburg National Military Park. In addition, by establishing a partnership between the Gettysburg Foundation and the National Constitution Center, the board ensured that a significant portion of the collection will be exhibited in Philadelphia.

In addition, the museum retained ownership of its archive of more than 10,000 documents, which are now housed at the Union League where they are available for research. Sharon Smith, president and chief executive of the Civil War Museum, explained that "We're running on fumes. There's virtually no money. We're down to a very small amount. That's why it's important to make sure all this is taken care of."[1] The museum board chair added, "As stewards of this world class collection, the Board of the Civil War Museum felt a strong ethical and historical responsibility to developing a partnership that would both protect this collection and ensure that it is accessible to the public and researchers in both Gettysburg and Philadelphia into the future."[2]

NOTES

1. Stephan Salisbury, "Civil War Museum Transfers Collection to Gettysburg with Constitution Center Exhibit Planned," *Philadelphia Inquirer*, May 3, 2016, accessed September 12, 2020, https://www.inquirer.com/philly/entertainment/arts/20160504_Civil_War_Museum_transfers_collection_to_Gettysburg_with_Constitution_Center_exhibit_planned.html.
2. "Civil War Museum of Philadelphia Announces Historic Agreement to Showcase World Class Collection," Civil War Museum of Philadelphia, Press Release, May 4, 2016, accessed September 12, 2020, http://civilwarmuseumphila.org/uploads/media_items/civil-war-museum-of-philadelphia-and-gettysburg-foundation-press-release-05-04-16.original.pdf.

AN UNPLANNED CLOSURE

I know that every museum understands the value of planning, but if you're still not convinced that you need to *plan* for closure, or have a formal Plan of Dissolution, there are a number of unfortunate examples of museums that have been forced to abruptly shut down with no warning to the public or even the staff, not knowing where the last months or weeks of funding will come from to pay the bills and staff, and with the most stressful and emotional experience for everyone involved. This is what happens when you *don't* plan:

CASE IN POINT:

Pasadena Museum of California Art, California

I had been executive director of the museum just a short time when I discovered there were serious problems (not only financial). I discussed them extensively with the board chairman, with the full board, and with the deputy director, conducting financial analyses and future projections. I arranged for two pro bono consultants: one to organize the financial accounting and reporting, and the other for strategic planning. We worked together to plan a board retreat a couple of months later, on March 24. We decided to present a fully transparent picture of the museum's problems (a detailed financial analysis, facility needs, legal concerns, and observations of the museum from donors), together with an overview of all the wonderful exhibitions, programs and catalogues published over the years, and positive organizational changes in the last three years (a delicate balance of sweet and sour). Then we presented four different options for the museum and discussed each of their financial and legal implications.

1. PMCA continues as an independent, nonprofit Museum
   a. remain at current location
   b. find another location
2. Close the Museum
3. Merge with another Institution
4. Sell the Museum[1]

The board had two weeks to ponder this and discuss until the next scheduled board meeting, when they unanimously agreed on option #1a. They felt energized, committed, and hopeful. This was success! But I was wrong. They were optimistic but also overwhelmed and surprised by the reality check. We drafted an Action Plan in April, which quickly became a Stabilization Plan because board members were not taking any action or making commitments. The Stabilization Plan stated:

> *In order to make a sound, data-based decision, further research and information must be gathered and certain actions taken. The Board agreed to set a plan in place that would result in its ability to make a more informed decision by July 1, 2019. As of May 10, insufficient progress has been made towards resolving that issue. The Board must realize that this is a crisis that needs to be addressed quickly. To that end, the suggestion is to revise the goal to make an informed decision by September 30, 2018.*

Then on June 11, I received a call from the board chairman, informing me that at our board meeting in two days, he would recommend that the museum close permanently. At the board meeting there were no questions about finances or fundraising prospects (even though the deputy director and director of development were present), no discussion of staffing or severance, and no communications plan. The board also did not ask the opinions of the three staff present (including me). The museum founders (who had two seats on the board) wanted to just turn off the lights and reopen later, but after changing their minds three more times in the next few months, they finally decided to dissolve. The board could not decide on the final closing date because they did not know where they would find the money to stay open even a couple more months, until the museum founders agreed to pay all closing expenses. There was no inventory list, and staff morale was very low as this was completely unexpected. The PMCA closed on October 31, 2018, with a reduced board (after revising the Bylaws) and no more staff. They received the final waiver from the Attorney General one year later.

NOTE

1. This was not really an option for the PMCA because it did not own the museum or office buildings (the museum founders did), and it had no permanent collection, so there were no assets to sell.

NOTES

1. "Causes of the Recent Financial and Economic Crisis: Testimony Before the Financial Crisis Inquiry Commission," Board of Governors of the Federal Reserve System (September 2, 2010) (statement of Ben S. Bernanke, Chair of the Federal Reserve System).

2. "How Sustainable Is Your Historic House Museum?" *History News* 63, no. 4 (Autumn 2008). Technical Leaflet #244, American Association for State and Local History, Historic House Affinity Group Committee, Technical Leaflet #244.

3. Susan Kenny Stevens, *Nonprofit Lifecycles; Stage-Based Wisdom for Nonprofit Capacity*, Long Lake, MN: Stagewise Enterprises, 2001.

4. "Guide for the Dissolution of California Nonprofit Public Benefit Corporations," Public Counsel, Community Development Project, January 2017, http://www.publiccounsel.org/tools/publications/files/0243.pdf.

5. This is not a legal term, just a way to discuss the more private nature of governance, funding, and operations that occurs with certain nonprofit museums that creates concern and often confusion over how the private and public elements of the museum best serve the interests of the public.

6. United States Senate Committee on Finance, "Hatch Concludes Review into Tax-Exempt Private Museums, Notes Concerning Findings," Chairman's News, June 2, 2016, accessed September 11, 2020, https://www.finance.senate.gov/chairmans-news/hatch-concludes-review-into-tax-exempt-private-museums-notes-concerning-findings.

7. American Planning Association, "Scenario Planning," accessed September 10, 2020, https://www.planning.org/knowledgebase/scenarioplanning/.

8. Two years earlier, the Center for the Future of Museums had commissioned its first discussion paper, "Museums & Society 2034: Trends and Potential Futures," that explored the challenges that society and museums would face in the next twenty-five years, focusing on demographic change, globalization, new forms of telecommunication, and new expectations about narrative and the consumption of culture. The report was prepared by Reach Advisors in December 2008. https://www.aam-us.org/wp-content/uploads/2017/12/Museums-Society-2034-Trends-and-Potential-Futures.pdf.

9. Elizabeth Merritt (Vice President, Strategic Foresight and Founding Director, Center for the Future of Museums), in discussion with the author, September 21, 2020.

10. "Ethics, Standards and Professional Practices: Questions and Answers about Selling Objects from the Collection," American Alliance of Museums, accessed September 18, 2020, https://www.aam-us.org/programs/ethics-standards-and-professional-practices/questions-and-answers-about-selling-objects-from-the-collection/.

11. John Wetenhall (Director, George Washington University Museum) reports that the building would have cost $10–15 million just to meet local codes and basic museum standards, in discussion with the author, September 29, 2020.

12. All other staff were given 60-day notices of layoff and told they could apply for other state positions. The administrative staff was fired, and the rest of the staff thought they would be losing their jobs too. Governor Rauner was anti-union. Staff

were allowed to continue to work until the lawsuit was settled, and ultimately a number of months later—the union (AFSCME) prevailed in court. Cinnamon Catlin-Legutko (current director of the Illinois State Museum), in discussion with the author, September 28, 2020.

13. Commission on Government Forecasting and Accountability, "Illinois State Museum," accessed September 28, 2020, https://cgfa.ilga.gov/resource.aspx?id=1822.

14. Catlin-Legutko, September 28, 2020.

15. "Shutdown Prevention and Economic Impact Issue Brief," American Alliance of Museums, 2019, https://www.aam-us.org/programs/advocacy/policy-issues/.

16. Joanna Woronkowicz et al., *Set in Stone: Building America's New Generation of Arts Facilities, 1994–2008* (Chicago: University of Chicago, Cultural Policy Center, 2012), 3–4, https://www.norc.org/PDFs/setinstone%20FINAL%20REPORT.pdf.

17. Ibid. "Capital projects put a tremendous amount of strain on organizations to raise money—an even greater amount of strain than they already have just to remain in operation. Therefore, in order to help alleviate this strain, many organizations tend to make unrealistic projections for earned revenue after the building project opens."

18. Ben Luke, "The Year in Museums: The Building Boom and the Expanding Canon," *Art Newspaper* XXV, no. 278, 5, April 2016, https://www.theartnewspaper.com/news/the-year-in-museums-the-building-boom-and-the-expanding-canon.

19. Alexandra Peers, "After the Building Boom," *Wall Street Journal*, October 30, 2008, accessed September 10, 2020, https://www.wsj.com/articles/SB122533230729582915.

20. "Museums that experienced financial trouble responded by reducing programming, but the built-in costs and revenues of these organizations made it more difficult and disruptive to reduce their program operating deficits by downsizing. We observed cutbacks and elimination of important ancillary programming such as education programs. Struggling museums also reduced or eliminated expensive special exhibitions that had often been booked years earlier, and focused instead on their permanent collections. Finally, museums would sometimes reduce their hours and the days on which they were open, or would perhaps darken part of the facility on a rotating basis." Woronkowicz et al., *Set in Stone*, 2012, 21.

21. Martha Morris, "Are Museums Recession Proof?," American Alliance of Museums, January 1, 2010, https://www.aam-us.org/2010/01/01/are-museums-recession-proof/. "The Theodore Roosevelt Museum in Oyster Bay, N.Y., for example, canceled its planned $90 million museum project, citing a drop in endowment and resulting operating cuts. The University of Arizona suspended work on a $130 million building planned to house its Science Center and State Museum in Tucson. After years of planning a new facility, the Children's Museum of Los Angeles declared bankruptcy when its major funder was charged by the U.S. Securities and Exchange Commission for investment fraud. And the Gulf Coast Art Museum in Largo, Fla., announced that it will give up plans for a new facility and close to the public."

22. Eileen Kinsella, "Cultural Institutions Spent a Whopping $7.9 Billion on New Buildings Last Year. Things Will Look Very Different in 2020." *Artnet News*, August 12, 2020, https://news.artnet.com/art-world/2019-cultural-buildings-8-billion-1901542.

23. John Wetenhall, "'Til Death Do Us Part . . .': Prenuptials for a Museum Merger," unpublished paper, September 2020.

24. Nina Siegal, "Many Museums Won't Survive the Virus. How Do You Close One Down?," *New York Times*, April 29, 2020, accessed April 29, 2020, https://www.nytimes.com/2020/04/29/arts/design/how-do-you-close-a-museum.html.

5

Step-by-Step Closing a Museum

Whether museums arrive at this point through careful planning over many months, or they suddenly find themselves overwhelmed by internal and/or external forces with no other choice, this chapter provides a detailed timeline of the steps needed to permanently close a museum and dissolve the 501(c)(3). Every museum comes to this same point via different roads, some windy and others straight, some long and others short, some smooth and paved and others very bumpy with potholes. If you are still in your planning stage, this chapter will help you to imagine the unfortunate scenario that you are now faced with permanent closure. This is what must happen.

First, the board decision. Unless the nonprofit is a membership-based organization, the decision must be made by the Board of Directors, by a majority vote, and the vote must be recorded in the official meeting minutes. Review your Articles of Incorporation and Bylaws for directions on who has the authority to vote for dissolution and any requirements for a vote, member or nonmember organization. Every 501(c)(3) nonprofit organization is required to have a Dissolution Clause, which is usually in its Articles of Incorporation. However, having a Dissolution Clause also in the Bylaws can provide more detailed information such as instructions on voting, as in this example:

Vote to Dissolve. The Corporation may be dissolved at any meeting of the Board of Directors, provided that: (1) a quorum is present; (2) the subject of the vote on dissolution was noted in the meeting announcement; and (3) the proposed dissolution has been a matter of formal discussion at the preceding meeting of the board.

As discussed in chapter 2, there are also legal requirements for how the Dissolution Resolution should be recorded and subsequently filed. Make sure that the board is clear in its vote about *how* it intends to close and *when*, and if it has the funds available to last until that time. This includes not only operations, but also severance payments and additional closure costs (more on those later). Include as many specific details as possible that you can decide on from the beginning. It is my belief that even if a quorum is present, the entire board should have an opportunity to vote by any means that are allowed according to the Bylaws (by email, telephone, proxy, or in person), given the significance of this decision. In the *Nonprofit Quarterly*, Lee Bruder (2017) raises the importance of where board meetings of this nature take place in the interest of "solid information management." He explains that "while we often advocate transparency, in this case we advise strict information control. A board and key staff should feel safe in exploring all issues without fear that the community or other staff will prematurely hear about plans that may never be implemented."

CASE IN POINT:

Pasadena Museum of California Art, California

At the Pasadena Museum of California Art, there were four board members absent at the June 13, 2018, meeting where the board chairman proposed to close the museum. This matter was not communicated to the full board prior to the meeting and was not included in the agenda. The board chairman called for a vote, but I insisted that they hold off until the four other board members were notified and given an opportunity to vote. Even though they argued that there was a majority present, they relented, and the vote was delayed for five days until all board members were notified. Two more votes came by email, and so there was a majority vote (two board members did not respond). The resolutions were:

1. The PMCA will close at the end of the Judy Chicago show on October 7, or possibly sooner, depending on the total financial commitment.
2. Staff will prepare the budget for remaining open until October 7, or as an alternative, closing at the end of July. The budget will include all costs including staff salaries, costs for opening and

closing the show, costs for any future commitments that must be honored, and the costs for an orderly disposition of the museum's obligations.

During those five days of waiting we had our final exhibition opening reception, and it was horrible having to keep the secret from everyone while smiling, giving speeches, and thanking donors and members. The hardest part, however, was with the staff. The day after the vote was final, I told the rest of the staff together in a morning meeting (the deputy director and director of development were present at the board meeting and also had to stay quiet). The staff was furious that I kept the news from them and felt betrayed. The board agreed on confidentiality until the vote was final, as did I, but there were consequences. Consider everything carefully when deciding whom to tell, how, when, and even where. The reality is that breaking this news is never easy, so be prepared.

Once your board has voted to dissolve, this is what must be done in terms of operations, in the order of priority. Make sure to review chapter 2 for the legal requirements.

Week One:

1. **Have the board designate someone to lead this process**. It should be the executive director or CEO, but if there is a problem with this person, then another staff person needs to be assigned. This person will work closely with the board chair, so preferably there should be one person from staff and one person from the board (does not have to be the chair). If you have the resources (or if you can identify pro bono), bring someone from the outside to facilitate this process, working closely with the staff point person and senior staff.
2. **Gather financial information**. These should have all been part of the board meeting discussions when the resolution was voted upon, but if not, work with your finance staff to get all the finances in order, specifically identifying current and past-due bills to pay and contractor obligations. Request reports: Statement of Financial Position, Statement of Activities, Statement of Cash Flows. You need to prove that the museum has no debts before the Attorney General can issue

a dissolution. Send a letter to all your creditors notifying them of the closure and give them 90 days to respond. You may be able to negotiate terms of payment or even a reduction in amount owed. Reach out to utility companies to see if they will agree to write off any portion of the total amount due, terminate any service contracts, and agree to any applicable termination fees. You should have an attorney to assist with these negotiations.

3. **Start working on an Operational Plan through the closure**. Confide in your deputy director, COO, or finance manager, and work together on this (although it is not necessary, or even advantageous, to agree on the best plan of action). Your plan will certainly be driven by your financial situation, but also by any legal and contractual restrictions, or changes in staffing. Present different plans to the board for approval: an extreme plan that cuts the most expenses (immediate staff layoffs with cuts to programming and museum hours, perhaps with the board taking over); a plan of continuity and appearances that retains all programming with regular hours of operation and minor staff cuts; and a moderate plan in between (see "Scenario Plans for Closure"). Make sure that you know which plan is your own recommendation, because the board will probably ask for it.

4. **Notify your museum association**. If you haven't done this already, immediately notify the American Alliance of Museums or your regional or state museum association. This is especially important if you are accredited by an association. Your professional associations are there to support you and provide resources and guidance during this time, so reach out to your network of colleagues. You never know what might come out of the network.

5. **Hire a lawyer with nonprofit experience**. If you already have an attorney or if there is one on the board, find out if they have nonprofit experience and ask if they have ever gone through the process of closing a nonprofit. If they have not, hire someone who has. I reached out to a local organization that supports nonprofits—Jericho Road—and they provided recommendations for nonprofit attorneys. There are also several organizations that provide pro bono legal assistance (or resources on where to find this service), such as Public Counsel, National Council of Nonprofits, and Community Action Program Legal Services, Inc. If you have the funds, it is highly recommendable to hire an outside attorney rather than use a board member, but often that is not possible due to a lack of funds. The attorney will advise on employee severance, review contractual obligations, and will handle the dissolution documentation and filing. You may also need to consider

other legal specialties depending on your circumstance; employment, inheritance, contracts, trusts, and to assist in negotiations with creditors if needed. Decide who will be the designated contact person to work with the attorney, usually a senior leader on staff.

6. **Craft a Communications Plan**. This plan should cover all internal (staff, volunteers, members, etc.) and external groups. Immediately request a statement from the board (this may take a few days or even a week). Draft a press release and get it approved by the board chair. Think about all your information channels—website, social media, e-newsletters—and make a strategic plan. Decide how you want to break the story, via which media outlet, and who you want to make available for interviews. I relied on the local newspaper, *Pasadena Star-News*, because I knew the editor, they had always supported the museum, and it just felt more like the museum to break the story locally. Be prepared because news travels fast in our digital age. Just before I notified staff in the late morning, I called the editor, because I knew that the news would quickly spread with the staff. By that afternoon, the story was in the online edition of the paper, and the next day it was in the print version. Think about who would appreciate knowing before it comes out in the news. If you already work with a public relations firm and have available funds, contact them immediately and rely on their ex-

Figure 5.1.   Communications Plan. Courtesy of author

pertise. Be proactive and not reactive. This plan should be approved by the board. If there is no time, then at least get the approval of the board chair and/or the board closure lead and share it with the entire board.

7. **Tell the staff**. The second you do this it will become public, but if you wait too long, the staff will be resentful that they were not told earlier. They will want to know everything (when is the closure, for how long will they keep their jobs, will programming still continue, why, etc.), but you probably won't have all the answers yet. They will go into shock and experience emotional trauma. Tell them all together at once (decide the best time of day, probably in the morning), then let them know that they can leave early for the day. You may not see them again for another couple of days, they may call in sick, and productivity will definitely drop. Allow everyone a few days paid time off. If possible, make a staff person available for counseling (usually Human Resources), and put aside funds for orders of pizza, donuts, coffee runs, and other treats to keep spirits up. Do not give them any details on staffing, severance pay, benefits, or scheduling until you are ready. If you have interns, include them in this meeting, and arrange to meet with each intern individually. Follow up with an email to all staff in case anybody is absent.

8. **Tell independent contractors and volunteers**. You can email them. Thank them all for all they do for the museum, tell them the facts as you know them, and that you will be following up with more details about works in progress and upcoming exhibitions and programs.

9. **Call donors**. Do not let your donors hear it from someone else first, or from the news. Let them know what is happening. Make sure you have first read all award letters, gift agreements, and naming-rights contracts to understand any funding requirements and restrictions. Let them know that you may need to schedule a meeting to discuss details. How will those funds be used? If they are for future programs or exhibitions, ask if they can be redirected toward your closure costs, or even to pay debts if possible. Are you in a position to repay any funds from foundations or public agencies if this is required? If you managed to secure new homes for your programs or exhibitions, ask the donor if those funds can be transferred to the new organization; and ask the new organization to recognize your donors and invite them to their exhibition events and openings.

10. **Decide on the final date of closure**. This is harder than it seems. The final date is usually dependent on your museum's financial situation, which is why the Operational Plan is critical to determining a closure budget. Other factors to consider are any contractual obligations for

current exhibitions and programming—how long will it take to cancel future exhibitions and programming, is there a complete and updated inventory of the collection and all the museum assets, and do objects need to be returned to lenders? Make sure that you distinguish between the date of public closure (this will be the one advertised to the public), and a later, final date when museum operations cease completely (and when the last staff leaves). The final, final date will be when the Attorney General grants a waiver of dissolution. The board must remain intact until that time.

11. **Talk to the press**. Know that you will be spending lots of time talking to the press—on the telephone for print, on the radio, on television, perhaps you decide to have a press conference—so get your story straight and stick to your Communications Plan. This is important—make sure that you are in a good mood when you talk to the press. Going through a closure is a very stressful time for everyone with lots of emotions ranging from sadness to anger to devastation and exhaustion, but you cannot show it to the press. Wear clothes that will make you feel good, remember to smile, and, most of all, remember that less is always more with the press, even with those journalists you know personally. Stick to your plan. Send out the press release after it has been approved by the board chair (or board closure lead). This may take time, as you want to include as many details as possible such as the final closure date. Press may even try to contact your current staff, so provide them with statements on what to say or not to say to the press.

12. **Think about your visitors**. Since you will still be open presumably for a short time, staff will be fielding all sorts of comments from the public. Tell them that they can always give their personal opinions, but if they don't want to, then they can just read a statement that you prepare for them (taken from the press release). Encourage staff to direct people to your website, where you will have that same statement and any updated information. Staff can also tell people to direct their comments and questions to your general info email, or to leave them on any paper comment cards or books (or digital screens) that you may have at the museum. At the PMCA, we repurposed old membership renewal cards that we found, and offered a space at the entrance for visitors to share their feelings. Some were positive and beautiful, and others very angry, but we kept them all up.

13. **Send out planned exhibition schedule to museums**. Quickly put together a list of your planned upcoming exhibitions and programs, then send the list to other museums and organizations that might be interested. Just provide the basics: description, dates, individuals

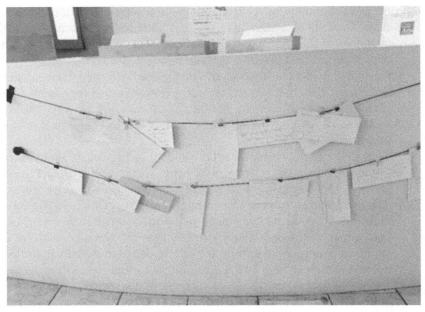

Figure 5.2.   REMEMBER Cards with Visitor Comments about the PMCA Closure. Photograph by author

involved, budget, resources needed, and if there is funding (see #9). If this an exhibition from your permanent collection and you will be distributing that collection, you need to first determine those recipient organizations before you finalize any arrangements for traveling exhibitions. Recipient organizations may appreciate having the extra time that works are traveling in order to prepare their storage facilities and galleries for incoming works.

14. **Send letters to major donors.** Prepare a formal letter from the board chair and the executive director/CEO, with the board statement, thanking them for their support, offering to be available to talk or meet, and providing as much detail as possible about the closure process and distribution of assets. If there are legal matters to resolve, such as naming of buildings or pledges or bequests, arrange a time to discuss these in person after consulting with an attorney.

15. **Contact all museum members**. When museum members start to hear the news, they will begin to call and ask about their membership, at all levels, so you need to decide quickly about membership. Together with your development or membership staff, go through your membership list and review all the benefits that you currently offer. Consider

how much longer you will stay open, and where your collections, exhibitions and/or programming are going. Consult with your attorney about tax-deductible benefits. Usually once someone has made a tax-deductible donation, that money cannot be returned to the donor because they have already declared the deduction. The donation was made while the museum was fully operating. Find ways to still make your members feel special. If you have a surplus left over of your branded materials (T-shirts, pens, mugs), or other items that you give to members, make them available to your members or higher-level members. If you have special store sales, give members early access or increase their discount. If your museum has a reciprocal museum program such as NARM or ROAM, those privileges can be extended past your closure date and through the end of their membership period, as long as members have a valid sticker on their membership cards. Even if you do not have all this information decided, send out a mass email to your members as soon as possible with a brief note, then you can follow up weekly with updates.

16. **Locate an inventory of the museum collection and all assets** (including office equipment, furniture, tools, museum store, books, vehicles, and more). If there is no inventory or if it has not been updated recently, assign staff to start working on this immediately. Include the following information: location of items, description, ownership or lender, donor or any associated funding, restrictions or instructions, and value. Make sure that the permanent collection has all the pertinent documentation such as certificates of ownership, provenance, condition reports, handling or exhibition instructions. Also include your *intangible* assets, such as donor database, mailing list, intellectual property, URL, logo, and even any signature programming you have that could be transferred or sold. Be prepared for items that suddenly go missing, whether part of the collection, store inventory, or office equipment. Pilfering does happen but it is hard to prove, which is why having a complete inventory in advance is so important. If you do not have proof of ownership documentation, examine the abandoned property laws in your state that could help to establish ownership. This could take time as well.

17. **Confirm Directors and Officers Insurance**, and that the policy is active through the closure period until the board is finally dissolved. Notify first your D&O insurance brokers of the closure, and later you will need to notify all other insurance brokers. Some policies have requirements for premiums and notifications, so review your policies carefully.

18. **Board communications**. Maintain regular communication between the director/CEO and the board, or at least with the board chair and/or the board closure lead. It is a good idea for senior staff to send regular email updates to the entire board. Depending on your timeline, full board meetings should be scheduled once a month instead of quarterly, or once a week instead of monthly for a smaller board. The board will need to approve a communications plan and an operational plan, hire outside counsel, and if they haven't already, they will need to decide how to distribute the assets and how to manage any debts. Remember that board members will also need help with responding to comments and questions about the closure, especially if they are not used to being the public face of the museum. As the news spreads, their friends and colleagues will approach them, and they will also need to be updated and have talking points that specifically state what remains confidential or can be publicly shared.

Whew, that was a lot for just one week! It may take more than one week to complete all these tasks, so get started on them right away. There will be delays in getting materials approved by the board and due to plunging staff productivity. Remember that your museum is a team that must work together at this time. All this work should not fall on the shoulders of just one person. If you can retain staff during the closure period, you need to justify to the board that they have essential tasks to carry out, so clearly identify those tasks.

Week Two:

1. **Continue to talk** with the press, funders, donors, members, and other museum directors and curators to take your exhibitions and programs.
2. **Communications**. Follow your Communications Plan. Continue to carefully monitor all social media with the appropriate messages, and to quickly deal with comments from disgruntled employees, angry museum members, or the public. Put a statement on your website and provide updates. Change any telephone messages and forward emails as staff begin to leave. Remember to find a way for the public (including members and donors) to contact staff, leave messages, and express their feelings, either through private or public channels.
3. **Be prepared for staff to be absent**. They may call in sick, productivity will drop dramatically, and they may stop working altogether on programs until they receive details from senior staff about the closure process (the wait may be due to board decisions). They may also be out looking for jobs and interviewing without saying so. Acknowledge this

from the beginning and offer flexible schedules to help staff find new jobs. Be prepared for lots of emotion from staff, ranging from anger to crying to confusion and desperation, and for lots of whispering around the drinking fountain, and be prepared for blame to be thrown around at the top, regardless of the circumstances of the closure. Continue to have Human Resources staff or someone else be available and reach out to staff with personal support and professional job seeking assistance with resumes and interviews. Find ways to motivate staff because you still must carry on operations until the very end. Board members may need to find time to meet directly with the full staff to help calm fears and anxieties; lighten the mood by serving refreshments.

4. **Meet with your attorney** to go through all the legal requirements, dissolution timeline, and any noteworthy concerns, and share this information with the board. Your attorney will start drafting documents but will need the board resolution with all the details, your complete inventory of assets with any accompanying legal paperwork, your Articles of Incorporation and Bylaws, and paperwork on any other nonprofit organization that may be associated with the museum. In going through your papers, you may discover surprises, such as a hidden nonprofit "Friends of the . . . Association" (as I did), which will also need to be formally dissolved. Your attorney will provide you with guidance regarding staffing, severance pay, donations, trusts, and other contractual matters.

5. **Conduct a financial analysis**. Work with your financial manager, CFO, or deputy director to create different financial models for the closure. There will be expenses for the closure, such as for attorneys, returning or transferring artwork, storage, severance pay for layoffs, increased security, and more. Make sure the board understands that staff cannot fundraise anymore and, in fact, that donations may need to be returned to donors, especially for restricted gifts and programs and exhibitions that may not take place. You may attempt to collect board dues or pledges, but do not expect every board member to be so enthusiastic about financially supporting a museum that is now closing. Collecting any receivables may be harder than usual. Think about other forms of revenue, such as closeout sales from your store or nonessential, unrestricted assets. Some book distributors will buy leftover exhibition catalogs at a discount, or other museum stores may be interested. Create a projected budget with receivables and payables, estimated cash to cover any liabilities, and a statement of activity. As soon as vendors hear about your closure, do not be surprised if they require full payment in advance of any services requested for the closure.

6. **Create a staffing plan**. Your operational plan was the first step to fig-
uring out how you will continue operating with your available funds,
but you should also have a separate and detailed staffing plan. First
review all the essential requirements for closure: de-installing any
exhibitions, condition reporting, returning works to lenders, inventory
and collections database, packing collection, maintenance and security,
store sales and returning consignments, financial accounting, notifications, and so forth. What staff do you need to complete these tasks? Just
as important is an assessment of the personalities and character of staff.
I cannot emphasize this enough: If you decide to reduce staff, make
sure that the remaining staff are reliable, trustworthy, hardworking,
cooperative, and have a positive attitude. This is not just a layoff to cut
expenses; in order to close a museum efficiently and responsibly, you
need the best team possible. Complicating your plan will be how long
staff has worked at the museum. Longtime staff have an institutional
memory that may be important as you compile information about your
collection and you may want to reward that loyalty by keeping them on
longer, but if you have newly hired staff, just imagine how devastating
this is to them, especially if they relocated for the job. Be prepared for
staff to suddenly resign because they found another job. Identify backup
staff that could take over their responsibilities, but also give staff the
opportunity to handle different tasks outside their job description. If
you have the resources, think about giving a bonus to the last remaining staff. Remember your part-time staff, outside consultants, and
independent contractors, and what roles they might play in completing
any essential closure tasks. Consult with an attorney first to avoid any
potential discrimination claims. This plan should be created and proposed by the CEO/director, but it should be shared with the board or
board closure lead.

7. **Reach out to your community**. By now you have spoken with the
press, your major donors, current funders, and members, but you also
need to contact your local public officials, neighbors, your local arts
and cultural organizations, and your program partners. Think about who
else you need to notify (former board members, mayor and public officials, neighborhood associations, local arts and culture organizations,
professional associations), what is the most appropriate method for each
(formal letter, email, telephone call), and prioritize your list because it
will take a while to get through it. Do you have Advisory Boards or Arts
Councils? They will probably have all heard the news and will want to
express their sympathy, their support, and to ask for details that you
may or may not have or be ready to share.

8. **Current exhibitions**. Contact lenders, who will be worried about the safety of their works and getting them back. If you have exhibitions that are traveling, contact future venues to discuss if they can assume the responsibility. Based on your public closure date, decide if the exhibition needs to be cut short or if it can complete its run. Assure your lenders that even after the public closure, staff will remain at the museum to arrange for de-installation, condition reports, packaging the works, and returning everything safely. Also confirm that the fine art insurance policy will be active until the very end. You may need to purchase an additional endorsement or extended period.

9. **Plan of distribution**. This is one of the most difficult parts of closing, which is why it should already be part of every museum's regular planning process. This topic is largely covered by the previous chapters that discussed legal and ethical considerations. Expect to receive requests from other nonprofits or museums offering to take your collection; you may even have galleries and auction houses call to see if you need help selling, and other individuals and nonprofits may be interested in buying or renting your building. All this may seem opportunistic, and you may feel angry in the moment, but they are also looking out for their own businesses and organizations, and it never hurts to keep an open mind. There have been cases of miracle donors appearing at the last minute to save the collection or the museum (see the discussion on crisis appeals in chapter 4). While the most obvious choice is another museum, think about your mission and history, and consider other nonprofits that provide a public benefit such as schools, community organizations, libraries, and foundations. Once you have decided on the recipient organizations, make introductions to your donors, especially those who have donated significant collections, in order to assuage donor concerns about continuing care and exhibition of their works.[1]

Stressful challenges tend to exaggerate the best and the worst of the human condition. Leaders can expect that during the process of dissolution, all aspects of organizational culture will heighten. The strengths and the trouble spots between individuals, roles and positions, and divisions and groups may need rapid, clear, and direct attention. Calming any rough internal waters as quickly as possible improves the potential for a successful outcome.

—Lee Bruder, *Nonprofit Quarterly*, 2017

I would say "resolving" instead of "calming any rough internal waters" because it might not be possible to quickly calm and repair what has been problematic at such a stressful time, and may have even led to this very closure. Definitely anticipate "rough waters" not only with staff, but also within the board, between staff and the board, with major donors, and in dealing with any larger organization such as a university, foundation, or corporation of which you may be a part.

Take care of yourself, remember to eat, drink water, and try to sleep. Take your vitamins and any immune-booster foods or supplements. Do whatever helps you relax—yoga, meditation, jogging, having a drink with a friend, walking your dog, cuddling up with your children—because you still have a long way to go, and you must stay healthy and alert for everyone at the museum, and also for yourself and your family.

Week Three:

1. **Closure plan**. Hopefully by now, the board has reviewed all the information and decided on a Closure Plan that can be shared with the public, as well as with staff.[2] The Closure Plan should include a financial analysis that confirms funding through the final dissolution period (which may last a year), the Staffing Plan and severance packages, the Communications Plan, and the Plan of Distribution. It should also include an Operational Plan with remaining public programming and exhibitions that are wrapping up, as well as any final closure events, private or public, and any other operational needs.

CLOSURE PLAN		
	Operational Plan	Closure budget, staffing, programs, public hours, additional needs
	Communications Plan	Press release, board statement, media strategy, prioritize contacts
	Plan of Dissolution	Distribution of assets
	Inventory	Complete and updated inventory of collection and assets, material and non-material
	Financial Analysis	Statements of Financial Position, Activities, and Cash Flows
	List of Exhibitions and Programs	Current and upcoming, including all lenders and donors, dates, and budgets
	Founding Documents	Articles of Incorporation, Bylaws (Dissolution Clause), Trust or other legal or historical documents

Figure 5.3. Closure Plan. Courtesy of author

2. **Send a press release**. This can only be done after the Closure Plan is finalized and you have more details on public hours of operation, programming, and the final date. It could be sent out earlier (a short media alert), but it could also go out later, depending on how quickly staff prepares the plans and how fast the board can reconvene and make a decision. You may need to consider sending out a second press release later when you have confirmed how your assets will be dispersed, where your collection will be going, and if any of your planned exhibitions and programs will take place at another museum.

3. **Begin staff layoffs**. Do it in person and together with another senior staff. For contract employees or temporary workers, send a letter in writing and follow up with a phone call. Your nonprofit attorney can draft all the termination papers (see Sample Documents), but you may encounter difficult situations, especially regarding general release agreements, confidentiality, and the return of keys and other museum equipment. As part of your financial analysis you should have determined severance pay depending on length of time at the museum, type of position, and other factors that should be discussed with your attorney. Seriously consider hiring an additional attorney that specializes in employment law to help with initial layoffs, because you do not want to scramble for legal advice when problems arise. Even though staff will be expecting this, and the reason for termination will be *Organization Layoff*, there will still be problems, and at the very least, lots of emotions. Even though the United States has at-will employment and all staff will eventually be laid off, deciding who leaves early and who stays until the very end is a delicate decision that was described in #4 from Week Two. An attorney will know your state labor laws and how to avoid discriminating based on disability, age, race/color, religion, sex, pregnancy, or national origin. Be prepared for staff who want to negotiate the terms of their severance package and may bring up old grievances, which is another reason to have an employment lawyer on hand. Let staff know that you can provide assistance with applying for unemployment.

4. **Look for art that is part of your physical property**. This could include murals, sculpture, installations, and functional art such as lighting fixtures or seating. Notify artists and check your legal responsibilities, especially if the art is integral to the building and cannot be removed. At the Pasadena Museum of California Art, the Los Angeles artist Kenny Scharf painted a mural (*Kosmic Krylon Garage*, 2004) all around the indoor garage walls. Our only legal requirement was to notify the artist, since the museum did not own the building, and the owners (the mu-

seum founders) had already put up the building for sale. The artist sent a crew to photograph the mural one last time. If the art can be removed, you have the responsibility to return it safely to the artist. If you own your building, will you sell or lease it, and how can you protect the art? If you do not, what will the owner do with it? This is your responsibility. The law in California (Civil Code §987) states in Chapter 3, Products of the Mind:

(h) (1) If a work of fine art cannot be removed from a building without substantial physical defacement, mutilation, alteration, or destruction of the work, the rights and duties created under this section, unless expressly reserved by an instrument in writing signed by the owner of the building, containing a legal description of the property and properly recorded, shall be deemed waived. The instrument, if properly recorded, shall be binding on subsequent owners of the building.

(2) If the owner of a building wishes to remove a work of fine art which is a part of the building but which can be removed from the building without substantial harm to the fine art, and in the course of or after removal, the owner intends to cause or allow the fine art to suffer physical defacement, mutilation, alteration, or destruction, the rights and duties created under this section shall apply unless the owner has diligently attempted without success to notify the artist, or, if the artist is deceased, his or her heir, beneficiary, devisee, or personal representative, in writing of his or her intended action affecting the work of fine art, or unless he or she did provide notice and that person failed within 90 days either to remove the work or to pay for its removal. If the work is removed at the expense of the artist, his or her heir, beneficiary, devisee, or personal representative, title to the fine art shall pass to that person.

(3) If a work of fine art can be removed from a building scheduled for demolition without substantial physical defacement, mutilation, alteration, or destruction of the work, and the owner of the building has notified the owner of the work of fine art of the scheduled demolition or the owner of the building is the owner of the work of fine art, and the owner of the work of fine art elects not to remove the work of fine art, the rights and duties created under this section shall apply, unless the owner of the building has diligently attempted without success to notify the artist, or, if the artist is deceased, his or her heir, beneficiary, devisee, or personal representative, in writing of the intended action affecting the work of fine art, or unless he or she did provide notice and that person failed within 90 days either to remove the work or to pay for its removal. If the work is removed at the expense of the artist, his or her heir, beneficiary, devisee, or personal representative, title to the fine art shall pass to that person.[3]

5. **Consider extra museum security**. You may have disgruntled staff or museum members, you may have a reduced staff, and there may be public protests. Remember that you still have a collection and building that you must protect and take care of in the public interest, in addition to protecting the staff. Security guards should be visibly recognizable from their clothing as they walk around the public areas of the museum. Make sure that you post emergency telephone numbers where staff can easily access them, and also email everyone the list. This is especially important as you may have unfamiliar people picking up items and helping with deliveries related to the closure.

6. **Archiving your museum**. As we discussed in chapter 3, what is the legacy of your museum? How will you preserve its history? Certainly, documents will accompany your collections and assets as they find new homes, and even your exhibitions and programs, but what about your organizational history? How will you archive the digital and physical documents of the museum? Where will you store them? What do you need to preserve of the museum for posterity, and for whom? Consider local universities and historical societies or museums. Look beyond your region if your museum specialized in something that is studied in a particular college or university, or even an independent institute. How will you archive your website, social media, your CRM database, and will there be somebody to monitor that digital archive? If you do not have this already, write down your museum history, accomplishments, societal contributions, and research (assign this to a staff member, volunteer, devoted member, or the board). Think about documenting this historical narrative with your local library or historical society, or even sharing it with other nonprofits to learn from your experience.

7. **Generating last-minute revenue**. First look for any donor restrictions on your assets. Even if there are no restrictions on major assets that donors have funded, such as vehicles, equipment, or furniture, you may want to notify your donor anyway beforehand. Legally, until museums receive their final waiver of dissolution from the state Attorney General, they cannot sell or distribute anything that is considered essential to the operations of the organization or that is a "substantial" amount of their assets. Museums must also ensure that buyers pay a reasonable amount, which is the "fair market value." Talk with your attorney and accountant if you intend to sell assets for the purpose of converting to cash to pay creditors, as this can be fraught with complications. What about your intangible assets? Will you sell your mailing list, or your programs and expert services? By now you have an updated inventory list and a good idea of where the collection and other assets will be

distributed. Hold discounted sales in your store. If you have a surplus of exhibition catalogs, contact other museums to sell in their stores or auction houses, sell at a discount, or at the very end, put all your catalogs on tables and invite teachers and other local nonprofits and community organizations to come and just take what they want. You can sell to pay for liabilities and debts, but you cannot end up with a surplus. This will be evident to the IRS in your final tax return 990.

8. **Plan your last day**. For your last day open to the public, consider offering free admission if you do not already, or hold a family day or a community-wide celebration together with all your partners, local artists, schools, and neighbors. If you still have an exhibition up, perhaps offer docent or curator-led tours. Think of how to make your museum members feel special, perhaps with an exclusive early opening or their choice of an extra catalog or branded materials. If you have the time, create a slide show or video of the museum that can play continuously, and offer all visitors a way to express their feelings and leave messages for staff and the board. You might also consider inviting the local media to garner some positive press at the very end.

While the entire closure process will take longer than three weeks, this is the most crucial time that very quickly becomes a whirlwind of activities, demands, emotions, and surprises, which is why it is better to think about all these details beforehand and to plan ahead as much as possible. Certainly, this does not cover the situation of every museum, but this gives you a general idea of the most important steps. There are certain tasks and decisions that can—and need—to be rushed, in order to best handle your financial situation, staff, donors, and your upcoming exhibitions and programs. But there are also other steps that you need to recognize and accept will take longer. Let your lawyer handle the legal requirements, let your accountant take care of getting all your financials in order, and the board should continue to take on responsibility and show leadership as long as it remains intact.

AFTER THE PUBLIC CLOSURE:

1. **Throw a party**. No, seriously. If there is any funding left (and do not ask for free catering or music this time), you should go out in style. The board ought to fund this last event if possible. Invite current and past donors, board members, artists or historians and curators that have been part of exhibitions, public officials, neighbors, and fellow

members of your local museum and cultural communities. I do not recommend inviting staff, other than those who are still working at the museum, since you will have already laid off most staff, which was certainly emotional and maybe even confrontational. If you invite just a few, then you might have to invite all past staff, which could be problematic. The board should speak (definitely the chair), and the director/ CEO. Thank everyone for their support of the museum over the years, reflect on your history, celebrate your achievements, recognize devoted individuals, and provide any details about the future of the collection, building, and exhibitions if possible. Use the same slide show as for your last public day, put up exhibition posters or banners on the

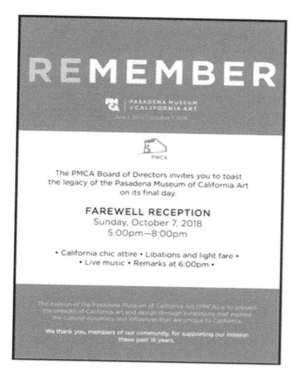

Figure 5.4. Invitation to the PMCA's Private Closing Party. Courtesy of author

walls if you have them. Hand out gift bags to each person (or couple) if you have leftover catalogs, postcards, or any branded materials.

2. **Keep an accountant.** Either arrange to keep your staff bookkeeper/ accountant on hand while waiting for the waiver, or hire an outside accounting firm. You will still need to file a final Form 990 Tax Re-

turn with the IRS within a few months of terminating the museum and should anticipate any additional expenses after the dissolution, as well as other accounting obligations such as year-end reports. If your museum solicited any donations in its last year of operation, that should also be included in your final 990. If you use accounting software such as QuickBooks, you will need to keep that account active until the very end, as well as any donor management or CRM software that records your donations.

3. **Keep the board**. By law, the board cannot dissolve until it receives the final waiver from the attorney general, which may take a while. Change your Bylaws to a minimum of three and ideally five board members (always an odd number), anticipating that there might be conflicts of interest or board members that need to recuse themselves or resign during this time. The rest of the board members must resign in writing but review your Bylaws for a Board Resignation clause.

4. **Website**. Decide how long to keep it active and who will be responsible for monitoring it, how it will be archived, and who will have access. This largely depends on how you have decided to distribute your collection and if you are transferring your programs and exhibitions. Any of the recipient organizations could agree to take over the website, either temporarily or permanently. It would be a great way to keep your collection accessible to the public, especially if it was already digitized on your website, along with archived exhibitions, any online catalogs, or related public programs such as audio or video content. Also consider other organizations that support your mission and whose constituents can benefit from this information. Do not forget to cancel your contracts for Web hosting and domain registration if you decide to shut down your website.

5. **Social media**. Decide when to stop all your social media accounts, and if you want to completely delete them or temporarily disable/deactivate. For the latter option, all data will be saved and you can restore the account later, which is preferable if your museum will be transferred or merged in some way. If you are completely dissolving your museum with no thought of reopening in any manner, then you want the former option, which is permanent and will not archive any data. You can request to first download data. Each social media site has its own procedures and it takes longer than you think; Facebook requires 90 days to completely delete, and Twitter takes 30 days (you can change your mind in that time). To mark your museum as permanently closed, you also need to change your business profile on Google Workspace or G Suite (for search and maps).

6. **Saving files**. If you have not found someone to take your paper archives, plan where you will store them, temporarily or indefinitely. Remember that you will need to save certain files until the final waiver is received from the Attorney General's office, which could take up to a year. After a certain period of time (see below) following the dissolution, these documents should be shredded, especially employee records. Check with your accountant, but for small businesses, the Internal Revenue Service recommends:

1. Keep records for 3 years if situations (4), (5), and (6) below do not apply to you.
2. Keep records for 3 years from the date you filed your original return or 2 years from the date you paid the tax, whichever is later, if you file a claim for credit or refund after you file your return.
3. Keep records for 7 years if you file a claim for a loss from worthless securities or bad debt deduction.
4. Keep records for 6 years if you do not report income that you should report, and it is more than 25% of the gross income shown on your return.
5. Keep records indefinitely if you do not file a return.
6. Keep records indefinitely if you file a fraudulent return.
7. Keep employment tax records for at least 4 years after the date that the tax becomes due or is paid, whichever is later.[4]

Figure 5.5. Last day, executive director's office and boxes of files. Photograph by author

7. **Distribution of assets**. You must safely maintain your collection and a "substantial" amount of your assets until you are legally allowed to distribute them to another nonprofit, unless you have received permission from the Attorney General to sell in order to cover your liabilities (or for any other reason). This will require you to keep them in your museum storage, or to find an outside storage that has the same proper conditions, which could be expensive. A suggestion is to consider giving all your assets to the organizations that you have already identified (and proposed to the Attorney General), with the understanding that transfer of ownership will come later with the waiver. You will need to create an itemized transfer document, signed by both parties.

8. **Utilities and services**. Set a date to cut each of the utilities (power, water, gas, telephone, internet), depending on your final closure date. If you have external services such as trash, cleaning, and security, also set a date to terminate these services. If you will store your collection or other assets inside the museum building until receiving the final waiver of disposition, then you should maintain electricity and security. Cancel any other services and accounts: cloud storage, subscriptions, mailing services, software, online payments, postal service, online surveys, internet security, online store, and so forth.

9. **Insurance**. Make a list of all your insurance policies: Fine Art, Directors & Officers Liability, General Liability, Workers Compensation, perhaps Automobile and Earthquake. You do not need Workers Compensation insurance after all staff have left the museum. Fine Art Insurance should stay active until you have distributed all the artwork, so check to see that you have extended the coverage period if necessary, and also General Liability if the collection remains at the museum or if people will need to enter the museum for any reason.

10. **Bank account**. Cancel the credit cards. Decide if you need to keep your bank account open to pay for the last remaining services (lawyers, accountants, storage if needed, D&O insurance), or to receive money from any sales. If so, then just keep your checking account open and make sure that one or two of the remaining board members are on that account. You need to notify your bank about the dissolution.

11. **Mailing address**. Consider opening a Post Office Box if you must close, sell, or vacate your museum building, and forward mail by requesting a change of address with the Postal Service. Another option is to have mail forwarded to the remaining board chair, board closure lead, or another remaining board member, while you are waiting to receive your final dissolution documents.

Reflect on not just *what* needs to be done at this time, but *how* you will do it, as a reflection of your museum's culture, history, and legacy. At the Pasadena Museum of California Art, board members made these statements while discussing the closure process: "Our goal should be to make this transition as smooth as possible realizing that we are impacting people's livelihood." "We want to go out on a high note." "We want to maintain dignity and our reputation with the least disruption to peoples' lives." How will your museum leaders (board and senior staff) ensure that this happens?

Ideally the closure process, much like normal museum operations, should be a collaboration between the director/CEO and the board chair. Decisions to permanently close, or any other alternative closure, should not be made by just one side without making the effort to consult with the other side. It is the board that takes the final resolution to dissolve and must sign the legal and financial documents, but it is the staff that handles the actual operations and can best make decisions about staffing, programming, funders, members, and more. The director/CEO should keep the board informed throughout the entire process and seek the board's advice for making important decisions. While the closure process largely falls on the shoulders of staff, think about what the board can do—talk to donors, community members, public officials, support and motivate the staff—and continue to guide the museum until the very end.

NOTES

1. With a clear understanding that the transfer of assets to the nonprofit is not finalized until the board receives the final waiver of dissolution from the Attorney General's office.

2. Each museum is different as far as how much of all this the board must approve or not. Remember that this is not just normal museum operations where there is a clear divide between staff and board responsibilities. At the very least, the full board should receive frequent updates on the closure, and the board closure lead and/or board chair should review all plans. Consult with your attorney to determine what documents, if any, the board must approve.

3. Chapter 3: Products of the Mind [980–989], California Legislative Information (enacted 1872, amended by Stats. 1994, effective January 1, 1995), http://leginfo .legislature.ca.gov/faces/codes_displaySection.xhtml?lawCode=CIV&section Num=987.

4. "How Long Should I Keep Records?" Internal Revenue Service, accessed September 15, 2020, https://www.irs.gov/businesses/small-businesses-self-employed/how-long-should-i-keep-records.

6

The Aftermath of Closure

Is there life after closure? We have seen how almost all museums indeed have some sort of afterlife, either in the history books (or books like these), if their archives are preserved, if they survive somehow through mergers or acquisitions, through their collections and publications, in articles that are written or in museum studies courses, or in the stories that former staff tell their colleagues. Gary N. Smith (2018), president of the Summerlee Foundation in Dallas, Texas, and its Texas History Program, writes how it is unrealistic to assume perpetuity in nonprofit organizations.

> A history organization that is founded, promotes and teaches history over a period of years, and helps to educate a new generation of local citizens should be deemed a success whether it eventually closes its doors or not. It may simply have reached the end of its mission's usefulness to its community, in which case, closing is not something to fear or be ashamed of.

But what about the individual afterlife? How do those individuals involved in a permanent closure recover, how does the experience affect them personally and professionally? I can say from personal experience that there is a definite stigma to having permanently closed a museum. Personal feelings of disappointment, failure, and defeat from having been the captain of a sinking ship make it difficult to jump back into the job market for another museum job, or even a board position. That optimism you once had may fade into cynicism and negativity, you overly scrutinize other museums and lose faith in their leaders (both staff and Boards of Directors). And when you do start looking for a new museum job, you sense an undeniable yet inexplicable and real reaction from people that confirms all your feelings. "Staff and board members who have struggled through the closure of a museum do not wear the scars from the ordeal lightly," admits Washington, DC–based journalist Amy Rogers Nazarov (2009).[1]

In the midst of a pandemic, museums and the entire professional field talk (and dream) about life after the pandemic, when there is a vaccine for all and museums are allowed to fully open again. Most people agree that museums will forever be changed after this crisis, and that there will be no return to exactly how things were before the pandemic. Such is life after closure. However, the essential question is, *how* will life be changed? Will you remain pessimistic, fearful of making bold actions and statements, with self-doubt and anger at others, or will you learn from the experience, help others through similar situations, and jump into the museum field again? *Mistakes Were Made* is an overwhelmingly popular session at the American Alliance of Museums' Annual Meeting that was started in 2012 by Sean Kelley, the senior vice president and director of interpretation at Eastern State Penitentiary Historic Site in Philadelphia. He was frustrated at the lack of honest discussion around failures at professional conferences, and explains:

> Contemplating mistakes helps us gather our thoughts and reflect on where, exactly, we went wrong. Admitting mistakes steels us against a repeat of the same error—the most painful of mistakes. These discussions allow others to gain from our painful experiences, and they encourage our colleagues to share their own cautionary tales for our benefit.[2]

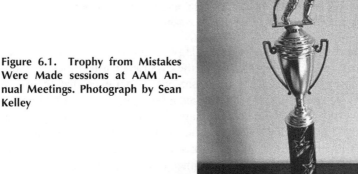

Figure 6.1. Trophy from Mistakes Were Made sessions at AAM Annual Meetings. Photograph by Sean Kelley

A look at for-profit businesses reveals a greater openness to dealing with closures and failures. The Bureau of Labor Statistics reports that about two-thirds of small businesses[3] with employees survive at least two years, about half survive at least five years, and only about one-third make it to ten years.[4] Furthermore, a study from Harvard Business School reveals that three out of every four venture-backed companies in the United States don't return investors' capital. The reasons are similar to why many nonprofits fail: "lack of focus, lack of motivation, commitment and passion, too much pride resulting in an unwillingness to see or listen, taking advice from the wrong people, lacking good mentorship, lack of general and domain-specific business knowledge (finance, operations, and marketing), raising too much money too soon."[5]

Entrepreneurs don't like to fail any more than museum directors and boards do, so they enter into start-ups or businesses understanding the risks, creating a business plan, and having exit strategies to rely on such as mergers and acquisitions, liquidation, buyouts, and IPOs (initial public offerings). The one major difference with museums is the private versus the public benefit. When a museum takes possession of buildings, collections, and charitable contributions on behalf of the public, to care for them all in posterity, it is justifiably hard to take risks, accept failure, and then move on to the next idea or project.

Yet the more we talk about failures, the more we learn from them and can celebrate smart risk-taking, bold decision-making, and innovation. Imagine talking about our failures in a way that would actually impress donors. We could explain how the staff came together as a team, how the director acted quickly and decisively, or how the museum skillfully adapted to change. You can position your museum—and those individuals involved—as being strong enough to face the challenge, to acknowledge weaknesses and mistakes, and to learn from experiences. One of the most popular job interview questions is, "Tell me about a time when you failed," because the response tells volumes about a person's character and potential to navigate a crisis.

In reflecting on the popularity of "Mistakes Were Made," Kelley said that, "Over time, I've come to think that the session isn't that effective in spurring critical thinking. The funniest story usually wins." People tend to blame others, he says, in a sort of "amused contempt" that does not often allow space for introspection and personal reckoning.[6] I am the first person to admit that I have blamed others for the PMCA closure, especially those that were in higher positions than I (the board) or former directors. It is human nature, it is emotional, and it should be short-lived. A good part of evaluation and critical thinking should be done individually, but the most important learning happens together with other museum colleagues and friends. Having these conversations creates an essential opportunity for everyone to express their feelings about what happened. Listen to others with different opinions, accept honest feedback, try to understand and not judge. The museum field is small, and a difficult closure experience can generate long-lasting friendships and professional relationships, if handled properly and with enough time.

This book has demonstrated the complexity of talking about closure. Not every closure is a permanent dissolution, and not every closure is a failure. Nevertheless, in retrospect, many museum closures could have been avoided or modified, which is what makes this reflective process so beneficial. But how do we get beyond the stigma of failure to have objective and meaningful conversations? Rick Collette, former chair of the Board of Trustees at the Bellevue Art Museum in Washington, admitted, "The decision to close was gut-wrenching, in terms of the ramifications to our community and the embarrassment that we had failed in our stewardship."[7] They closed with the hope of reopening the museum, which did happen eighteen months later, with a new artistic focus, new funding, building renovations, and renewed community support. "To close the museum was a difficult thing, but it was the right thing. And because of that, the museum will be much stronger," said board member Ronald Bayley.[8] Nonprofit attorney Una Jost confirms that museums can legally amend the purposes set forth in their Articles of Incorporation to a modified or completely different charitable purpose in order to engage in new public benefit activities.

British academics Stephen Graham and Nigel Thrift (2007) write about breakdowns and disruptions in society, noting that "repair and maintenance" are more significant because they are "the means by which society produces learning, adaptation and improvisation. But when things break down, new solutions may be invented. Indeed, there is some evidence to suggest that this kind of piece-by-piece adaptation is a leading cause of innovation, acting as a continuous feedback loop of experimentation which, through many small increments in practical knowledge, can produce large changes."[9] They cite the phenomenologist Martin Heidegger (1889–1976) and his concept of *vorhanden* (objectively present) in asserting that, "Things only come into visible focus as things when they become inoperable—they break or stutter and they then become the object of attention."[10]

Adaptation can be understood within the context of "saving" a museum before closure, as this book has described various closure alternatives such as mergers, acquisitions, scaling down, and repurposing of historic houses. Yet dissolution itself is an important transformation as well. If museums approach this major change with responsibility, planning, respect for legal requirements, and all the care and consideration for public benefit that were taken to operate the museum all its years, then the closure might be regarded as opening up new opportunities. "Yet often what is preserved is not the identity of the museum itself, but a shadow of its memory in the scattered objects and archived name." In a bittersweet article in *Hyperallergic* (September 20, 2013) titled "Resting in Pieces: The Scattered Fate of Closed Museums," Allison C. Meier cites numerous examples of museums with an aftermath, but laments that they never regain their original context, "the broader story of which they were once a part."[11]

It has been the objective of this book to guide museums through the very difficult process of dissolution, and more importantly, to emphasize the need for careful planning, foresight, and open dialogue. Every museum comes to a point—and each museum knows its own point—when the final decision must be made about the fate of the museum, when you stop planning to save and start the closure process, when the public benefit is best served through dissolution. Hopefully all the tips, questions, and resources in this book, as well as the various case studies, will facilitate these decisions. And always remember, there is life after closure, for the museum, for the collections, and for everyone involved.

NOTES

1. Amy Rogers Nazarov, "Ethical Considerations for Museum Closures," American Alliance of Museums, Mission & Institutional Planning, July 1, 2009, https://www.aam-us.org/2009/07/01/ethical-considerations-for-museum-closures/.

2. Sean Kelley, "Mistakes Were Made and Survived," *INSITE Magazine*, Museums Australia Victoria, September/October 2013, 3.

3. The Small Business Administration categorizes businesses as "small" depending on each sector. For Arts, Entertainment and Recreation, a small business has no more than $7.5 million to $38.5 million in average annual receipts depending on the subsector. Sean Peek, "How to Know if You Really Classify as a Small Business," *Business News Daily*, August 4, 2020.

4. "Do Economic or Industry Factors Affect Business Survival?," Small Business Administration, Office of Advocacy, June 2012.

5. Deborah Gage, "The Venture Capital Secret: 3 Out of 4 Start-Ups Fail," *Wall Street Journal,* September 20, 2012.

6. Sean Kelley (Senior Vice President, Director of Interpretation, Eastern State Penitentiary Historic Site), in discussion with the author, September 30, 2020.

7. Rogers Nazarov, "Ethical Considerations."

8. Natalie Singer, "Bellevue Arts [sic] Museum Set to Reopen in Late Spring," *Seattle Times*, April 2, 2005.

9. Stephen Graham and Nigel Thrift, "Out of Order: Understanding Repair and Maintenance," *Theory, Culture & Society* 24, no. 3 (2007): 1–25.

10. Ibid., 2.

11. Allison C. Meier, "Resting in Pieces: The Scattered Fate of Closed Museums," *Hyperallergic*, September 20, 2013, https://hyperallergic.com/84447/resting-in-pieces-the-scattered-fate-of-closed-museums/.

Appendix

Sample Documents

1. Dissolution Resolution
2. Officer Certificate of Board Action
3. Notice of Reduction in Force
4. Scenario Plan for Downsizing Operations
5. Settlement Agreement and General Release
6. Termination Letter
7. Termination Certificate
8. Supplemental Termination Certificate
9. Employee Nondisclosure and Intellectual Property Assignment Agreement
10. Scenario Worksheet for Your Museum
    Elizabeth Merritt, AAM Center for the Future of Museums
11. Compliance Report for Financially Motivated Disposal of Items from a Museum Collection
    Museums Association, UK

1. Dissolution Resolution

[NAME OF MUSEUM]

A [STATE] NONPROFIT PUBLIC BENEFIT CORPORATION

MINUTES OF A REGULAR
MEETING OF THE BOARD OF DIRECTORS

A regular meeting of the Board of Directors of the [Museum Name], a [State] nonprofit public benefit corporation, was held at the time, on the day, and at the place set forth as follows:

Time:	
Date:	
Place:	

The following directors were present, constituting a quorum for the meeting:

-
-
-
-
-
-
-
-
-
-

The following directors were absent:

-
-
-

The following directors participated in the meeting by conference telephone through which all persons participating in the meeting could hear and speak to one another:

-
-
-

The following individuals were also present at the invitation of the directors:

-
-

[Name] served as chair of the meeting, and [Name] served as secretary of the meeting and kept the minutes for it.

The chair called the meeting to order and announced that the meeting was held pursuant to a fixed resolution of the Board pursuant to Section XXX of the Corporation's Restated Bylaws.

The minutes of the last meeting, which were mailed electronically to the members of the Board, were approved as presented.

I. AGREEMENT TO WIND UP AND DISSOLVE

The Chair proposed that it is in the best interests of [Museum Name] to be wound up and dissolved. Discussion followed. After motion duly made, seconded, and carried unanimously in favor and none opposing, the following resolutions were adopted:

WHEREAS, the Board of Directors has determined that it is in the best interests of the Corporation that this Corporation be wound up and dissolved.

WHEREAS this Corporation has no members and *Corporations Code* §XXXX permits such a nonprofit corporation to elect to voluntarily wind up and dissolve by approval of its Board of Directors.

RESOLVED, the Officers and Directors of this Corporation are authorized and directed to take appropriate measures to wind up and dissolve this Corporation.

RESOLVED, the President and Secretary of this Corporation or a majority of the Directors currently in office are authorized and directed to execute and verify a Certificate of Election to Wind Up and Dissolve in accordance with *Corporations Code* §XXXX, to file the Certificate with the [State] Secretary of State, and to file a copy of that Certificate with the [State] Attorney General.

RESOLVED, that, on commencement of proceedings to wind up the Corporation, the Officers of this Corporation are authorized and directed to prepare and file such other documents and take such other action as may be necessary or advisable in connection with the winding up and dissolution of the Corporation.

RESOLVED, that the Officers of this Corporation are authorized and directed to file all final returns with the [State] Franchise Tax Board.

PLAN OF DISTRIBUTION OF ASSETS

The Corporation currently holds the cash and other assets listed in **Exhibit "A"** to this resolution, and the Corporation is able to pay or provide for all its known debts and liabilities.

RESOLVED, that all known debts and liabilities of the Corporation be provided for or paid.

RESOLVED, that after (1) paying or adequately providing for all its known debts and liabilities, and (2) complying with *Corporations Code* §XXXX, *i.e.*, securing the Attorney General's written waiver of objections to the disposition, the Corporation assets described in Exhibit "A" remaining on hand shall be distributed, in conformity with this Corporation's articles of incorporation, to _____, a [State] Nonprofit Public Benefit Corporation. [Describe which assets go to which entity]

RESOLVED, that the President and Secretary of this Corporation are authorized, empowered, and directed to execute and deliver in the name of and on behalf of the Corporation such deeds, assignments, or other instruments of transfer as may be deemed necessary or proper and the Officers and Directors of this Corporation are authorized, empowered, and directed to do any and all acts and things necessary to carry out, perform, implement, and consummate the above-described distribution and to wind up the corporate affairs and dissolve this Corporation, including, but not limited to, filing a Certificate of Dissolution in accordance with *Corporations Code* § XXXX.

II. AMENDMENT TO RESTATED BYLAWS AND REMOVAL OF DIRECTORS

The Chair proposed that it is in the best interests of [Museum Name] to amend the Corporation's Restated Bylaws decreasing the minimum directors required to be on the Board in light of the Board's agreement for the Corporation to wind up and dissolve. Discussion followed. After motion duly made, seconded, and carried unanimously in favor and none opposing, the following resolutions were adopted:

WHEREAS, the Board of Directors has reviewed the proposed Amendment to Restated Bylaws attached as Exhibit A and approve of the same without modification.

RESOLVED, that the proposed Amendment to Restated Bylaws attached as **Exhibit B** is hereby approved.

RESOLVED, that the Secretary of the Corporation is authorized and directed to execute a certificate of the adoption of those Amendment to Restated Bylaws, to insert them as so certified in the minute book of the Corporation, and to ensure that a copy of the Amendment to Restated Bylaws, similarly certified, is kept at the principal office for the transaction of business of the Corporation.

III. RESIGNATION OF DIRECTORS

Certain Board members informed the Board of their desire to resign from the Board in light of the Board's agreement for the Corporation to wind up and dissolve. Discussion followed. After motion duly made, seconded, and carried unanimously in favor and none opposing, the following resolutions were adopted:

WHEREAS, the following Board members have relayed their desire to resign from the Board in light of the Board's agreement for the Corporation to wind up and dissolve.

RESOLVED, the Board accepts the resignation of the following Board members with gratitude for their service to the Corporation: [Insert Names]

There being no further business, the meeting was, on motion duly made and seconded, adjourned at [Insert Ending Time].

Respectfully submitted,

Date: [Date]

_____

[Name]

Secretary of the [Museum Name],

a [State] nonprofit public benefit corporation

Appendix: Sample Documents

EXHIBIT A

LIST OF ASSETS OF [MUSEUM NAME]

LIST OF ASSETS OF [MUSEUM NAME]

-
-
-
-

EXHIBIT B

AMENDMENT TO NO. 1 TO RESTATED BYLAWS

AMENDMENT TO NO. 1 TO RESTATED BYLAWS

This Amendment No. 1 amends the Restated Bylaws of the [Museum Name], a [State] nonprofit corporation, adopted by the Board of Directors on_____, as follows:

Section 2.1 of the Restated Bylaws is hereby amended by deleting the text of Section 2.1 and inserting the following section in its place:

Section 2.1 Number; Composition. This Corporation shall have a Board consisting of at least five (5) but no more than thirty-five (35) directors unless changed by amendment to these Bylaws. The exact number of directors shall be fixed, within the limits specified, by amendment of the next sentence duly adopted by the Board. The exact number of directors shall be five (5), until changed as provided in this Section.

Except as hereby amended, the Bylaws shall remain in full force and effect.

CERTIFICATE OF SECRETARY

I, the undersigned, the duly elected Secretary of the [Museum Name], a [State] nonprofit corporation, do hereby certify:

That the foregoing Amendment to Restated Bylaws, consisting of one (1) page was adopted as the Amendment to Restated Bylaws of the Corporation by the directors of the Corporation on [Date]; and the same do now constitute the Amendment to Restated Bylaws of said Corporation.

IN WITNESS WHEREOF, I have hereunto subscribed my name this day of _____.

_____

[Name]

Secretary

2. Officer Certificate of Board Action

[NAME OF CHARITY]

OFFICER'S CERTIFICATE

I, [Name of Officer], being the duly elected, qualified and acting [Name of Office] of [Museum Name] certify and affirm on behalf of [Museum Name] as follows [*select one*].

[IN THE CASE OF AN ACTION
TAKEN AT A MEETING (IN PERSON OR TELEPHONIC).]

At a duly noticed and held meeting of the [board of directors/trustees or members] held on [*insert date*] during which a quorum was present and acting that the following resolution was duly authorized consistent with the provisions of XXXXX, §XXX and said authorization has not in any way been amended, annulled, revoked, or repealed and remains in full force and effect as of the date hereof:

OR

[IN THE CASE OF AN ACTION TAKEN
BY UNANIMOUS WRITTEN CONSENT.]

In an action by written consent of the [board of directors/trustees or members] effective [*insert date*], that the following resolution was duly authorized consistent with the provisions of XXXXX, §XXX and said authorization has not in any way been amended, annulled, revoked, or repealed and remains in full force and effect as of the date hereof:

1. VOTED: That [Museum Name] be voluntarily dissolved by the preparation and presentation of a dissolution petition and other necessary documents, on such terms as are approved by the [officers, directors, or members] to *[select one]*
   [if no assets] the Office of the Attorney General of [State], pursuant to XXXXX, §XXX.

OR

   [if assets will remain] the Office of the Attorney General of [State] and the Supreme Judicial Court, pursuant to XXXXX, §XXX.
2. VOTED: That the officers of [Museum Name] be and hereby are each authorized, empowered and directed in the name of [Museum Name] to execute and deliver any and all documents to any other regulatory agency, including but not limited to, the Secretary of the [State], the Internal Revenue Service, and the [State] Department of Revenue, and to do all things which they, in their discretion, seem necessary or advisable to implement the foregoing resolutions.

[INCLUDE ONLY IF THE ORGANIZATION HAS REMAINING ASSETS TO TRANSFER.]

3. VOTED: That the officers of [Museum Name] hereby authorize the transfer of all remaining assets, after the payment of all debts and liabilities, namely *[briefly describe the type of assets, e.g., cash, stock, real estate, etc.,]* to [Name of Receiving Entity] after approval by the Supreme Judicial Court, for the following purpose *[insert whether for general or restricted purpose and why]*.

Signed under the pains and penalties of perjury.

_____

Name

Name of Office

Date:

3. Notice of Reduction in Force

Date:
To: All _____ Employees
From:

As you may be aware, on [date], at a meeting of the [museum name], Board Chairman [name] recommended that the Museum close after the current exhibitions end on [date]. The vote was made final on [date] and the following day, Executive Director [name] informed the museum staff and made the public announcement. The Board of Directors released the following statement:

> The Board of Directors would like to thank all of the donors, contributors, lenders, museum members, and especially our hard working, dedicated staff who have made this wonderful adventure possible.

As a result of the Board's [date] decision, the Museum will be eliminating various jobs and terminating the employment of many employees at the Museum. Affected employees will be informed by their managers. Employee layoffs will commence on [date], and we anticipate that all affected employees will be separated from the Museum on or about [date], or within fourteen (14) days thereafter.

The Museum expects this workforce reduction to be permanent.

We know this will create hardship for those being laid off. We want to accomplish this reduction in force as fairly and compassionately as possible, and we will seek to provide you with what support and assistance we can in the transition.

We will provide you details regarding the layoff, including information on options regarding benefits and other information no later than [date].

For further information, please contact [name], Deputy Director of Operations at the following: [email], tel. [telephone number].

4. Scenario Plan for Downsizing Operations

CURRENT SALARY ANALYSIS AND OTHER PAYOUT ITEMS

		Executive Director	Deputy Director	Development	Marketing
Based on last two pay dates	Current staff models & totals	[Name]	[Name]	[Name]	[Name]
Monthly salaries & estimated part-time wages, including taxes	$	$	$	$	$
Health insurance	$	$	$	$	$
Current monthly salaries, taxes, & health insurance expense	$	$	$	$	$
Vacation payouts for accruals through [Date]	$	$	$	$	$
Severance pay	$	$	$	$	$

BIG PICTURE TASKS FOR COMPLETION BY DEPARTMENT

Executive Director	Deputy Director	Development	Marketing

Exhibitions	Education	Facilities	Gallery Part-Time No Vacation/Insurance
[Name]	[Name]	[Name]	[Names]
$	$	$	$
$	$	$	$
$	$	$	$
$	$	$	$
$	$	$	$

Exhibitions	Education	Facilities	Gallery Part-Time No Vacation/Insurance

Option 1–MOST DRASTIC				
• Immediate layoffs for designated areas • Reduce balance of administrative staff to part-time • Change gallery & store operation days to Fri–Sun • Valid for closure end of [Date]	*Executive Director*	*Deputy Director*	*Development*	*Marketing*
	Lay off, pay out vacation, board member step in to oversee closing or hire/contract someone to execute closure plan	Lay off, contract with CPA for accounting & payroll only, no management of HR, insurance, or store and gallery	Lay off after resolution plan completed with donors and members, pay-out vacation, benefits expire [Date]	Reduce work schedule to part-time to match revised operations closure plan—24 hrs/week
Option 2				
• Selected layoffs, estimated [Date] • Admin absorb responsibilities • Cut operations of gallery & store to Fri–Sun • Valid for closure end of [Date]	*Executive Director*	*Deputy Director*	*Development*	*Marketing*
	Absorb final development, membership, and exhibitions (also hire temp)	No schedule change	Lay off by [Date]	Absorb education/outreach, partial store, manage interim events, assist with limited operations
Option 3:				
• Cut operations and full-time staff to part-time Wed–Fri for administrative staff, Fri–Sun for gallery & store • Continue health benefits for those subscribed • Valid for closure end of [Date]	*Executive Director*	*Deputy Director*	*Development*	*Marketing*
	Reduce hours to 3 days/week	Reduce hours to 3 days/week	Reduce hours to 3 days/week	Reduce hours to 3 days/week
Option 4				
• No program cuts, full monthly schedule • Minor personnel cuts and temps to hire • Minimal schedule reductions/changes • Valid for closure end of [Date]	*Executive Director*	*Deputy Director*	*Development*	*Marketing*
	Absorb some exhibition tasks, no schedule change	No schedule change	Reduce to 32 hrs/week, exit [Date] or earlier	Absorb store events, online shop, inventory, & reporting Possible reduction to 32 hrs/week
COST SAVINGS				
Current monthly salaries, taxes, & health insurance expenses per option	$	$	$	$
Revised monthly staff & expenses per option	$	$	$	$
Potential monthly savings per option (does not include vacation/ severance)	$	$	$	$

Exhibitions	Education	Facilities	Gallery Part-Time No Vacation/Insurance
Lay off by [Date], payout vacation, pay benefits thru [Date], bring in temp exhibition person to coordinate final deinstallation and returns	Reduce work schedule to part-time to match revised operations closure plan—24 hrs/week, continue benefits	Layoff by [Date], payout vacation, pay benefits thru [Date], hire temp to handle repairs, maintenance, & janitorial functions	Redesign schedule to accommodate revised operating schedule of museum, restructure by keeping employees able to work new set schedule and lay off those who cannot
Exhibitions	Education	Facilities	Gallery Part-Time No Vacation/Insurance
Lay off by [Date], hire temp labor for limited hours and term	Lay off by [Date]	Lay off by [Date], hire temp labor for limited hours and term	Fri–Sun (3-day work week)
Exhibitions	Education	Facilities	Gallery Part-Time No Vacation/Insurance
Reduce hours to 3 days/week	Reduce hours to 3 days/week	Reduce hours to 3 days/week	Reduce hours to 3 days/week
Exhibitions	Education	Facilities	Gallery Part-Time No Vacation/Insurance
Possible reduction to 32 hrs/week	Reduce to 32 hrs/week	Hire temp for 3 days/week	Downsize gallery attendants until final closure, supplement with volunteers 25–29 hrs/week each
$	$	$	$
$	$	$	$
$	$	$	$

5. Settlement Agreement and General Release

This Settlement Agreement and General Release (this "Agreement"), dated as of [Date], is entered into by and between the [Museum Name], a [State] Nonprofit Corporation (the "Employer") and [Name] (the "Employee").

RECITALS

A. Employee rendered services to Employer from [Date] until [Date]. Employee was employed as [Title]. Employer has discontinued using Employee's services because of a layoff.

B. The parties wish to avoid any further dispute regarding Employee's services. The parties have therefore negotiated a full and final settlement of all differences between them through the date of this Agreement.

C. The parties hereby memorialize that settlement as set forth below.

NOW, THEREFORE, for good and valuable consideration, the receipt and sufficiency of which is hereby acknowledged, Employer and Employee agree as follows:

1. *Payment to Employee.* Provided that Employee has executed this Agreement and the attached Employee Nondisclosure and Intellectual Property Assignment Agreement, Employer agrees to pay to Employee the gross sum of **[Amount in writing] ($Amount)** (equal to two (2) weeks' severance pay, less standard withholding and authorized deductions, for a net check of **[Amount in writing] ($Amount)** as full and complete settlement of a disputed claim. Employer shall issue to Employee an IRS Form W-2 regarding

this payment. Plaintiff shall hold harmless and indemnify Defendant from any adverse tax consequences that may arise from this characterization.

2. *Release.* Employee, on behalf of Employee and Employee's representatives, heirs, successors, and assigns, does hereby completely release and forever discharge Employer, including its related or affiliated companies, partnerships, subsidiaries, and other business entities and its and their present and former respective officers, directors, shareholders, owners, agents, employees, representatives, insurers, attorneys, successors, and assigns (referred to collectively as the "Released Parties"), from and against all claims, rights, demands, actions, obligations, liabilities, and causes of action, of any and every kind, nature, and character whatsoever, that Employee has now, has ever had, or may have in the future against the Released Parties, or any of them, based on any acts or omissions by the Released Parties, or any of them, as of the date of the execution of this Agreement by Employee, including, without limitation, any and all claims arising out of Employee's rendering of services to Employer or the termination of Employee's services, including, without limitation, any and all claims, whether based on tort, contract, or any federal, state, or local law, statute, or regulation or based on or related to the Age Discrimination in Employment Act (29 USC §§621–634); Title VII of the Civil Rights Act of 1964 (42 USC §§2000e—2000e–17), as amended by the Civil Rights Act of 1991 (42 USC §§1981–1988); the Americans with Disabilities Act of 1990 (42 USC §§12101–12213); or the [State] Fair Employment and Housing Act ([State] *Government Code* §§XXXX–XXXX) (referred to collectively as the "Released Claims"), to the fullest extent allowed at law. The Released Claims do not include those that the law does not allow Employee to release. Notwithstanding the foregoing, Employee agrees to waive the right to recover monetary damages in any charge, complaint, or lawsuit filed by Employee or anyone else on Employee's behalf for any Released Claims.

3. *No Legal Action.* Employee represents that Employee has not filed, initiated, or caused to be filed or initiated any legal action covering any Released Claim and agrees that Employee will never file, initiate, or cause to be filed or initiated, at any time after the execution of this Agreement, any claim, charge, suit, complaint, action, or cause of action, in any state or federal court or before any state or federal administrative agency, based in whole or in part on any Released Claim. Further, Employee shall not participate, assist, or cooperate in any suit, action, or proceeding against or regarding the Released Parties, or any of them, unless compelled to do so by law.

4. *Release Full and Final.* Employee understands and agrees that this is a full and final release covering all unknown and unanticipated injuries, debts, claims, or damages to Employee that may have arisen or may arise in connection with any act or omission by the Released Parties before the date of execution of this Agreement. For that reason, Employee hereby waives any and all rights or benefits that he or she may have under the terms of [State] *Civil Code* §XXXX, which provides as follows:

> "A general release does not extend to claims which the creditor does not know or suspect to exist in his or her favor at the time of executing the release, which, if known to him or her, must have materially affected his or her settlement with the debtor."

5. *Costs and Expenses.* Except as provided in Paragraph 1 above, the parties agree that each party shall be responsible for the payment of his, her, or its own costs, attorney fees, and all other expenses in connection with the negotiation of this Agreement or any of the Released Claims.

6. *No Admission of Liability.* It is understood and agreed that this is a compromise settlement of doubtful and disputed claims, or potential disputed claims, and the furnishing of the consideration for this Agreement shall not be deemed or construed as an admission of liability or responsibility at any time for any purpose. It is further agreed and understood that this compromise and Agreement are being entered into solely for the purpose of avoiding further expense and inconvenience from defending against any or all of the Released Claims. Employer expressly denies liability for any and all Released Claims.

7. *Terms and Conditions Confidential.* Each party agrees to hold the terms and conditions of this Agreement in strict confidence. Employee shall not disclose the terms and conditions of this Agreement to any past or present employee of Employer or to any other individual except Employee's attorneys, accountants, tax consultants, state or federal authorities, or as may be required by law. Any person to whom disclosure of the terms and conditions of this Agreement is made in accordance with this Paragraph 7 shall be instructed that the terms and conditions of this Agreement are confidential. In the event that an inquiry is made to any of the parties by any individual, other than the individuals described in this Paragraph 7, to whom the parties are bound or required to disclose such information, regarding the status of the dispute between the parties, the parties may comment only that this dispute was "resolved." No party shall disparage any other party, nor shall any party make any public statement nor do any act that is calculated or likely to result in an inquiry by any member of the public as to any aspect of the dispute

Appendix: Sample Documents

between the parties or any of the information covered by this confidentiality provision. All parties shall make their best efforts in all respects and in good faith to keep all information concerning the dispute between the parties or any of the information covered by this confidentiality provision confidential and secret from any person except the individuals described in this paragraph to whom the parties are legally bound or otherwise required or permitted to disclose such information.

8. *No Further Access to Premises.* Employee understands and agrees that he may not return to the Employer's place of business at any time for any reason or commit any violation of Employer's policy.

9. *Inquiries.* Any inquiry to Employer about Employee shall be referred to the then-current Personnel Director, who will only state that Employee was employed as [Title] from [Date] through [Date], and that Employer's policy does not permit further discussion about its employees.

10. *Liquidated Damages.* The parties acknowledge and agree that the provisions of Paragraphs 7, 8, and 9 are material considerations and that neither of them would have entered into this Agreement but for their inclusion in this Agreement. The parties therefore agree that, in the event a court of competent jurisdiction finds that either party has breached the provisions of Paragraphs 7, 8, and 9, it would be extremely difficult or impracticable to fix the actual damages of the other party and that, on the basis of the facts and circumstances known to them at the time of this Agreement, on such a finding of breach, the breaching party shall pay to the non-breaching party as liquidated damages and not as a penalty the sum of Two Thousand One Hundred Fifteen Dollars and Thirty-Nine Cents ($2115.39) per occurrence, which represents reasonable compensation for the loss incurred because of such breach.

11. *Wages; Work-Related Injuries.* Employee hereby acknowledges that all wages accrued to the time of employment termination have been paid to Employee by Employer and that there has been no unreported work-related injury through the date of this Agreement.

12. *Counterparts.* This Agreement may be executed in one or more counterparts or duplicate originals, all of which, taken together, shall constitute one and the same instrument. Facsimile or electronic signatures shall be equally binding as originals.

13. *No Reliance; Consideration.* The undersigned parties each acknowledge that they have entered into this Agreement voluntarily, without coercion, and on the basis of their own judgment and not in reliance on any representation or promises made by the other party, other than those contained in this Agreement. This Agreement recites the sole consideration for the promises exchanged in this Agreement. Each party has read this Agreement and is fully aware of its contents and legal effect.

14. *Legality; Survival; Binding Effect.* If any one or more of the provisions of this Agreement is held to be invalid, illegal, or unenforceable, the validity, legality, and enforceability of the remaining provisions shall not be affected or impaired thereby. This Agreement shall survive the performance of the specific arrangement herein. This Agreement is binding on and shall inure to the benefit of the parties and their respective heirs, executors, administrators, successors, and assigns.

15. *Amendments; Integration; Headings.* The parties understand and agree that this Agreement may be amended or modified only by a signed writing and may not be amended or modified orally. This Agreement incorporates the entire understanding and agreement of the parties concerning its subject matter and supersedes all prior agreements and understandings concerning such subject matter. The headings of this Agreement are for convenience of reference only and shall not limit the interpretation of this Agreement.

16. *Authority.* Each person executing this Agreement on behalf of a corporation or other legal entity warrants that he or she holds the position indicated beneath his or her signature and that he or she has been duly authorized by the corporation or other legal entity to execute this Agreement on its behalf.

17. *Governing Law.* This Agreement shall be governed by and construed in accordance with the internal laws of the State of [State], without regard to conflict-of-law principles.

18. *Right to Consider Before Signing; Right to Revoke.* Under the Older Workers Benefit Protection Act of 1990, Employee is advised as follows:

(a) that Employee should consult an attorney regarding this Agreement before executing it;

(b) that Employee has twenty (21) days from the date that this Agreement is presented to Employee in which to consider this Agreement and whether he or she will enter into it, although Employee may, in the exercise of Employee's own discretion, sign or reject it at any time before the 21-day period expires;

(c) that, at any time within seven (7) days after executing this Agreement, Employee may revoke the Agreement by contacting [Name of Deputy Director of Operations], [Museum Name], [Address], phone number [Telephone number];

(d) that this Agreement is not enforceable until the revocation period has passed.

[EMPLOYEE NAME]
(Signature) _____

Date: _____

[MUSEUM NAME],
a [State] Nonprofit Corporation
By: (Signature) _____   **By: (Signature)** _____
Name: [Name] _____   **Name: [Name]** _____
Its: Deputy Director of   **Its: Executive Director** _____
Operations _____   **Date** _____
Date _____

6. Termination Letter

[Date]
[Name]
[Address]
Dear [Name]:

We want to wish you the best of luck in your future endeavors. We appreciate your contributions to the [Museum Name] (the "Organization") and thank you for the efforts you made on our behalf.

Further to our meeting of [Date], this is to confirm that your employment with the Organization is terminated effective as of [Date]. As stated at our meeting on [Date], the reason for termination of your employment is as follows:

ORGANIZATION LAYOFF

1. This is to remind you that you need to return any Organization property, car, and equipment in your possession, and submit any approved expense claims.
2. Your final pay is calculated as of [Date] and includes all unpaid wages and all accrued but unused vacation pay. This will acknowledge that we are delivering or have already delivered to you your final paycheck.
3. With your final paycheck, you will receive a Settlement Agreement and General Release. When you return this signed to the Organization's Deputy Director of Operations [Name], you will receive a check for severance pay.

4. In parting, we want to want to remind you of your continuing obligations under your Employee Nondisclosure and Intellectual Property Assignment Agreement, a copy of which is enclosed for your review.

The agreement requires that you deliver to us all Confidential Information in your possession relating to the programs and activities of the Organization, including all originals, copies, translations, notes, or any other form of said material, without retaining any copy or duplicates thereof, and promptly to delete or destroy any and all written, printed, electronic, or other material or information derived from the Confidential Information.

The agreement further obligates you to not use or disclose Confidential Information, in whole or in part, for any purpose other than in performing your duties to Organization within the course and scope of your employment with the Organization. The agreement also obligates you to keep confidential all Confidential Information and to preserve the confidential and proprietary nature of the Confidential Information at all times.

Please refer again to the Employee Nondisclosure and Intellectual Property Assignment Agreement for the complete terms of your obligations. Your former position with the Organization put you in a position to have significant confidential information. We trust that you will deal with that information, and your contractual obligations generally, with the utmost responsibility and honor. We remind you that you agreed that we may share this agreement with any future employer.

5. Information concerning your options regarding your benefits of employment, such as COBRA rights to continue your medical insurance coverage, will be mailed to your home separately.

6. Information regarding unemployment insurance benefits can be found in the [State] State Employee Development Department's publication *"For Your Benefit: [State]'s Programs for the Unemployed* (DE 2320)," available online at: [Website].

7. Information regarding the [State] Department of Health Care Services' "Health Insurance Premium Payment (HIPP) Program" is also available online at: [Website].

8. We have also enclosed a Termination Certificate for your signature and a self-addressed stamped envelope for you to return your signed Termination Certificate to us. Please sign, date, and return the copy of this letter enclosed as confirmation of receipt of this letter and enclosures.

9. Outplacement assistance is available to those who request it. Please contact [Name], phone number [Telephone number] to participate.

Again, best of luck in your future endeavors.

Very truly yours,

[MUSEUM NAME]

a [State] Nonprofit Corporation

By: _____

Name: [Name]

Its: Deputy Director of Operations

RECEIVED:

By: _____

Name: [Name]

Date: [Date]

Enclosures:

- Employee Nondisclosure and Intellectual Property Assignment Agreement
- Settlement Agreement and General Release
- Termination Certificate
- Termination Checklist

7. Termination Certificate

I certify as follows:

1. When I signed acknowledging receipt of the Employee Handbook of the [Museum Name] (the "Employee Handbook"), I read and understood it. I have fully complied with the terms of the Employee Handbook, including, without limitation the following provisions:

- *Discipline and Standards of Conduct*
  The following conduct is prohibited and will not be tolerated by the Museum. . . .
  Prohibited Conduct
  . . .
  - *Stealing or removing, without permission, Museum property, or property of another employee, or a visitor.*
  . . .
  - *Breach of confidentiality of personnel information.*
  - *Violations involving the non-disclosure agreement or failure to maintain the confidentiality of the Museum's proprietary information.*
  - *Engaging in any conduct which is not in the best interest of the Museum.*
- *Confidentiality*
  Each employee is responsible for safeguarding confidential information obtained in connection with his or her employment. In the course of doing work, employees may have access to confidential information regarding the Museum, its suppliers, its visitors or perhaps even fellow employees. It is the employee's responsibility to in no way reveal or divulge any such information unless it is necessary to do so in the per-

165

formance of his or her duties. Access to confidential information should be on a "need-to-know" basis and must be authorized by the employee's supervisor. Any breach of this policy will not be tolerated and legal action may be taken by the Museum.

- **Technology Systems**
  The Museum provides an e-mail system, voice mail system, access to the internet and other technology systems to assist employees in conducting Museum business. All information, data, and messages created, received, sent, or stored in these systems are, at all times, the property of the Museum. No software may be placed on Museum computers that has not been authorized and is not work related. No employee may copy computer programs or other files from the Museum equipment for personal use or transmit them to an unauthorized third party. This includes correspondence, databases, visitor files, and custom developed software. Unauthorized duplication of digital files will be considered theft and may cause termination and/or prosecution. The foregoing systems are to be used primarily for Museum related purposes. All existing Museum policies apply to employee conduct on the internet and use of all technology systems, including, but not limited to, Museum policies regarding intellectual property, misuse of Museum property, discrimination, harassment, sexual harassment, information and data security and confidentiality.

2. I recognize that the unauthorized taking of any of the Organization's Confidential Information is a crime under [State] *Penal Code* §XXX and that any unauthorized taking of the Organization's Confidential Information may also result in civil liability against me under [State] *Civil Code* §§XXXX–XXXX.

3. I understand that the Organization may notify my new employer regarding the terms of the Employee Handbook and the general nature or subject matter of the Confidential Information (without actually disclosing any Confidential Information) to which I had access while employed by the Organization.

4. I further agree that for twelve (12) months from this date, I will not solicit, induce, recruit, or encourage any of the Organization's employees to leave their employment nor improperly use any Confidential Information of the Organization.

Date: _____   _____

                                        [Employee Name]

8. Supplemental Termination Certificate

I certify as follows:

1. When I signed the Employee Nondisclosure and Intellectual Property Assignment Agreement (the "Confidentiality Agreement"), I read and understood it. I have now reviewed the Agreement again and certify that I fully understand its terms and my continuing obligations under it, with which I promise to comply.

2. I have fully complied with the terms of the Confidentiality Agreement, including, without limitation, the return of any documents and other tangible materials of any nature pertaining to my employment with the [Museum Name] (the "Organization"), including all Confidential Information (as defined in the Confidentiality Agreement) of the Organization. I further represent that I do not possess, and have destroyed, deleted, or discarded, any Confidential Information of the Organization that may have existed in either tangible form or digital or electronic form outside of the workplace, such as on any Internet server, computer hard drive, computer diskette, CD, USB or Zip drive, tablet, smart phone, or other mobile device, that I have personally utilized, maintained, or kept during the course of my employment with the Organization. I also represent that I have not, during the time of my employment, ever sent or given such Confidential Information to any third person or party without the knowledge and express authorization of the Organization's management. I understand and acknowledge that should I fail to comply with my obligations under the Agreement, the Organization has the right to obtain an injunction against me, including, without limitation, an injunction prohibiting me from disclosing Confidential Information to a third party.

3. I recognize that the unauthorized taking of any of the Organization's Confidential Information is a crime under [State] *Penal Code* §XXX and that

any unauthorized taking of the Organization's Confidential Information may also result in civil liability against me under [State] *Civil Code* §§XXXX–XXXX.

4. I understand that the Organization may notify my new employer regarding the terms of the Confidentiality Agreement and the general nature or subject matter of the Confidential Information (without actually disclosing any Confidential Information) to which I had access while employed by the Organization.

5. I further agree that for twelve (12) months from this date, I will not solicit, induce, recruit, or encourage any of the Organization's employees to leave their employment nor improperly use any Confidential Information of the Organization.

Date: _____   _____

                                          [Name]

9. Employee Nondisclosure and Intellectual Property Assignment Agreement

[MUSEUM NAME]

A [STATE] NONPROFIT CORPORATION

EMPLOYEE NONDISCLOSURE AND

INTELLECTUAL PROPERTY ASSIGNMENT AGREEMENT

This Nondisclosure and Intellectual Property Assignment Agreement (this "Confidentiality Agreement") with an effective date of [Date] (the "Effective Date), is entered into between **[Museum Name]**, a [State] nonprofit corporation ("Organization"), and **[Name]** ("Employee") with respect to the following:

A. Organization possesses considerable know-how and proprietary intellectual property rights relating to, without limitation, copyrights to the web, print, and/or video materials produced by Organization staff and volunteers, in furtherance of the Organization's mission to [Museum Mission].

B. Organization and Employee have entered into this Agreement to assure the confidentiality of information provided by Organization to Employee, generated by Employee, or of which Employee otherwise becomes aware.

NOW, THEREFORE, for good and valuable consideration, the receipt and sufficiency of which are hereby acknowledged, the parties agree as follows:

1. DEFINITION OF CONFIDENTIAL INFORMATION. The term "Confidential Information" as used in this Agreement means all information disclosed by Organization to Employee, as well as any information to which Employee has access or that is learned, generated, or created by Employee, whether alone or jointly with others. Confidential Information includes, but is not limited to, source code and programming information, and all promotional, operational, technical, economic, or financial knowledge, information, or data of any nature whatsoever relating to the programs and activities of Organization, which has been or may hereafter be learned, generated, created, or otherwise obtained by Employee, alone or jointly with others, whether in written, electronic, oral, or any other form. Confidential Information shall also include any information that is provided to Organization by third parties and is subject to obligations of confidentiality.

2. EXCEPTIONS TO DEFINITION OF CONFIDENTIAL INFORMATION.
Confidential Information shall not include the following:

(a) Information that is publicly available at the time of disclosure, or information that later becomes publicly available through no act or omission of Employee;

(b) Information that Employee can demonstrate was in Employee's possession before the date of commencement of Employee's employment with Organization; or

(c) Information disclosed to Employee by a third party not in violation of any obligation of confidentiality to Organization.

3. DISCLOSURE AND USE OF CONFIDENTIAL INFORMATION. Employee shall use the Confidential Information only for the purpose of performing Employee's duties to Organization within the course and scope of Employee's employment, and shall make no use or disclosure of the Confidential Information, in whole or in part, for any other purpose. Employee agrees to keep confidential all Confidential Information and to preserve the confidential and proprietary nature of the Confidential Information at all times. Further, Employee acknowledges that from time to time Organization is entrusted with confidential information of third parties and agrees to abide by the terms of any nondisclosure agreements entered into between the Organization and such third parties.

4. NO OWNERSHIP OR OTHER RIGHTS GRANTED. All right, title, and interest in and to Confidential Information shall remain the property of Organization. Nothing in this Agreement shall be construed to grant Employee any rights to or license under the Confidential Information or under any related patent, patent application, trademark, copyright, know-how, or other intellectual property of Organization.

5. REQUIRED DISCLOSURE. In the event that Employee is requested or required by subpoena or other court order to disclose any Confidential Information received pursuant to this Agreement, it is agreed that Employee shall provide immediate notice of such request(s) to Organization and shall use reasonable efforts to resist disclosure, until an appropriate protective order may be sought, or a waiver of compliance with the provisions of this Agreement granted. If, in the absence of a protective order or the receipt of a waiver hereunder, Employee is nonetheless, in the written opinion of its counsel, legally required to disclose Confidential Information received pursuant to this Agreement, then in such event Employee may disclose such information without liability hereunder, provided that Organization has been given a reasonable opportunity to review the text of such disclosure before it is made and that disclosure is limited to only the Confidential Information specifically required to be disclosed.

6. RETURN OF INFORMATION. Employee agrees to return all Confidential Information in Employee's possession on termination of Employee's employment with the Organization for any reason, or upon any earlier written request from Organization, including all originals, copies, translations, notes, or any other form of said material, without retaining any copy or duplicates thereof, and promptly to delete or destroy any and all written, printed, electronic, or other material or information derived from the Confidential Information.

7. NATURE OF INFORMATION. Employee acknowledges and agrees that the Confidential Information protected by this Agreement is of a special, unique, unusual, extraordinary, and intellectual character; that money damages would not be sufficient to avoid or compensate for the unauthorized use or disclosure of the Confidential Information; and that specific performance, injunctive relief, and other equitable relief would be appropriate to prevent any actual or threatened use or disclosure of the Confidential Information. Employee also acknowledges that the interests of Organization in its Confidential Information may be irreparably injured by disclosure of such Confidential Information. The remedies stated above may be pursued in addition to any other remedies available at law or in equity for breach of this Agreement, and Employee agrees to waive any requirement for the securing or posting of any bond in connection with such remedy. Should litigation be instituted to enforce any provision of this Agreement, the prevailing party shall be entitled to recover all costs, including without limitation reasonable legal fees, cost of investigation, and cost of settlement.

8. WORK FOR HIRE. Employee understands and agrees that, to the extent permitted by law, all work, papers, reports, documentation, drawings, images, product ideas, service ideas, photographs, negatives, tapes and masters, computer programs (including their source code and object code), prototypes, and other materials (collectively, "Work Product"), including, without limitation, any and all such Work Product generated and maintained on any form of electronic media, that Employee generates, either alone or jointly with others, during employment with Organization shall be consid-ered a "work made for hire," and ownership of any and all copyrights in any and all such Work Product shall belong to Organization. In the event that any portion of the Work Product should be deemed not to be a "work made for hire" for any reason, Employee hereby assigns, conveys, transfers, and grants, and agrees to assign, convey, transfer, and grant to Organization all of Employee's right, title, and interest in and to the Work Product and any copyright therein, and agrees to cooperate with Organization in the execution of appropriate instruments assigning and evidencing such ownership rights under this Agreement. Employee hereby waives any claim or right under the doctrine of "droit moral" (moral right) to object to Organization's copyright in or use of the Work Product.

9. INVENTIONS. Employee hereby assigns and agrees to assign to Orga-nization all of Employee's right, title, and interest in and to any discoveries, inventions, and improvements (collectively, Inventions), whether patentable or not, that Employee makes, conceives, or suggests, either alone or jointly with others, while employed by Organization. Any Invention that was made, conceived, or suggested by Employee, either solely or jointly with others, within one (1) year following termination of employment with Organization and that pertains to any Confidential Information or business activity of Or-ganization shall be irrebuttably presumed to have been made, conceived, or suggested in the course of Employee's employment and with the use of the time, materials, or facilities of Organization. This Paragraph does not apply to any invention that qualifies under Section 2870 of the [*State*] *Labor Code,* a copy of which is attached hereto as ***Exhibit A***.

10. ASSISTANCE. Employee shall assist Organization and any person designated by it in every proper way and at Organization's expense to reg-ister, obtain, and enforce Organization's rights in Work Product and Inven-tions. Such assistance shall include, but not be limited to, assistance with and execution of, as applicable, registrations and applications for patent, copyright, or other intellectual property rights in any and all jurisdictions, and execution of further evidence of Employee's assignment of Employee's rights under this Agreement.

11. DISCLOSURE OF INVENTIONS. Employee hereby agrees to disclose promptly all Inventions to Organization and to perform, during and after Employee's employment, all acts deemed necessary or desirable by Organization to permit and assist Organization, at its expense, in obtain-ing and enforcing the full benefits, enjoyment, rights, and title of and to the Inventions throughout the world. Such acts may include, without limitation, the execution and delivery of documents and the provision of assistance or cooperation in legal proceedings. In addition, Employee hereby irrevocably designates and appoints Organization and its duly authorized officers and agents as Employee's agent and attorney-in-fact, to act for and in Employee's behalf and stead to execute and file any such applications and to perform all other lawfully permitted acts to further the securing of Organization's rights in and to the Inventions.

12. AT-WILL EMPLOYMENT. Employee acknowledges and agrees that Employee's employment with Organization is at will and, therefore, may be terminated by Employee or by Organization at any time, with or without cause and with or without notice. The at-will employment relationship shall remain in effect throughout Employee's employment with Organization, unless modified by an express written contract for a specified term signed by Employee and an authorized representative of Organization. The at-will employment relationship may not be modified by any oral or implied agreement.

13. GOVERNING LAW. [State] law shall govern the interpretation of this Agreement, without reference to rules regarding conflicts of law. Any dispute arising out of this Agreement shall be submitted to a state or federal court sitting in XXXXXX County, [State], which shall have the exclusive jurisdiction regarding the dispute and to whose jurisdiction the parties irrevocably submit.

14. NO OTHER AGREEMENT. This Agreement, together with its Exhibit A, constitutes the parties' entire agreement with respect to the treatment of Confidential Information by Employee and supersedes any and all prior statements or agreements, both written and oral. This Agreement may be amended only by a writing signed by the parties. This Agreement does not replace or supersede any confidentiality provisions in the Organization's Employment Handbook as amended from time to time; to the contrary, all are important components of the Organization's commitment to protecting the Organization's Confidential Information.

15. SURVIVAL. This Agreement (a) shall survive Employee's employment with Organization, (b) is personal to Employee and may not be assigned by Employee, (c) may be assigned by Organization in its sole discretion and shall inure to the benefit of the successors and assigns of Organization, and (d) is binding on Employee's heirs and legal representatives. If Employee's employment with Organization is terminated for any reason, Employee consents to the Organization's notification of Employee's obligations under this Agreement to any subsequent employer.

16. NO WAIVER. No waiver of any term, provision, or condition of this Agreement, whether by conduct or otherwise, in any one or more instances, shall be deemed to be or be construed as a further or continuing waiver of any such term, provision, or condition or as a waiver of any other term, provision, or condition of this Agreement.

17. SEVERABILITY. If any court of competent jurisdiction determines any provision of this Agreement to be invalid or unenforceable, such provision shall be interpreted to the maximum extent to which it is valid and enforceable, all as determined by such court in such action, and the remaining provisions of this Agreement shall, nevertheless, continue in full force and effect without being impaired or invalidated in any way.

IN WITNESS WHEREOF, the parties hereto have entered into this Agreement on the day and year first written above.

EMPLOYEE NAME|
(Signature) _____
Date: _____

[MUSEUM NAME],
a [STATE] Nonprofit Corporation
By: (Signature) _____   **By: (Signature)** _____
Name: [Name] _____   **Name: [Name]** _____
Its: Deputy Director of Operations Its: Executive Director

_____   _____
Date: _____   **Date:** _____

EXHIBIT A

[STATE] LABOR CODE §XXXX

(a) Any provision in an employment agreement which provides that an employee shall assign, or offer to assign, any of his or her rights in an invention to his or her employer shall not apply to an invention that the employee developed entirely on his or her own time without using the employer's equipment, supplies, facilities, or trade secret information except for those inventions that either:

1. Relate at the time of conception or reduction to practice of the invention to the employer's business, or actual or demonstrably anticipated research or development of the employer; or
2. Result from any work performed by the employee for the employer.

(b) To the extent a provision in an employment agreement purports to require an employee to assign an invention otherwise excluded from being required to be assigned under subdivision (a), the provision is against the public policy of this state and is unenforceable.

10. Scenario Worksheet for Your Museum

Elizabeth Merritt, AAM Center for the Future of Museums

The worksheet below provides some prompts for creating tailored scenarios. These prompts are just a starting point. You may, for example, want to add more financial detail to inform critical decision-making about staffing and operations. You may want to add story elements that explore impacts particular to your institution (e.g., pausing a capital campaign or construction project). Complete the worksheet for each of the scenarios framed above—low, medium, and high impact. I recommend you write from the perspective of a year from now, looking back to tell the story of how you successfully navigated this difficult year.

HOW OUR MUSEUM SURVIVED THE _____ CRISIS

In this future . . . [Complete for each scenario: low/medium/high impact]

- We were closed for a total of ____ months, and reopened on _____
- The income streams that sustained us through 2020 and 2021 were ____
- The following funders/donors stepped in to support us _____ in the following ways (e.g., with additional funding or easing of grant restrictions)_____
- ____ staff members were furloughed/laid off (specify which) in ____, and by ____, ___ had been rehired.
- We applied for financial relief from these government programs or charitable funds _____
- We cancelled these events and exhibitions_____
- We instituted these online/digital events and programs_____

- We cultivated members and donors by_____
- Our total operating losses in 2020 were $____ (Deficit at the end of the year)
- The museum's investments went from $____ at the beginning of 2020 to $____ at the end of the year.
- Our donors and funders see the museum as having played a critical role in supporting our community in the past year, because we _____

Start by choosing key variables that will set the stage for each scenario. These currently unknown quantities will have significant influence on your operating environment and decisions. Identifying the most critical things you need to know will help you focus your attention and filter the overwhelming amount of information crossing your news feeds. For example, your key variables might include:

- Pattern of COVID-19 epidemiology (severity, timeline, pattern of cycling)
- Length and extent of state and local closures and distancing orders
  ○ Business closures
  ○ School closures
- Overall impact on your local economy, including employment
- Available relief funding (locally and nationally for museums or individuals)
- Public willingness to attend museums after restrictions are lifted
- Metrics about your organization, e.g.:
  ○ Current operating reserves (cash on hand to pay expenses)
  ○ Financial health of the museum's sponsors, funders, and donors
  ○ Membership renewals
  ○ Financial impact of cancellations in 2020—penalties incurred or revenue lost from contracts, bookings, etc.
  ○ Value of the museum's investments
  ○ Total financial impact to the museum's operations

Next, find sources of information that will help you fill in values for each of these variables as events play out. Complement this external data with your museum's key financial indicators and other pertinent data. For each of these scenarios, sketch out what is happening at your museum. What is your most likely financial outlook? How have you found additional sources of support?

11. Compliance Report for Financially Motivated Disposal of Items from a Museum Collection

Museums Association, UK

Museums should complete a Compliance Report if:

- **They have been requested to do so by the Museums Association (MA) and the relevant Accreditation Assessing Organisation (AAO).**
- **They have read Appendix 4 of the Disposal Toolkit and undertaken all or most of the actions in stages 1–3.**

The Disposal Toolkit and Appendix 4: Additional guidance for museums on financially motivated disposal can be found at: www.museumsassociation .org/collections/sale-of-collections.

The information provided in this form, together with any supporting evidence, will be used by the MA's Ethics Committee and the AAO to form a view on whether the proposed sale meets the requirements of the MA's Code of Ethics and the Accreditation Standard. It may take several months from date of submission of the Compliance Report for either organisation to be able take a formal view on the proposed sale.

Please submit the completed Compliance Report to:

[Insert relevant contact details of the MA and each AAO]

If you require any advice or assistance in completing the Compliance Report please contact the MA or your relevant AAO.

Confidentiality

The Museums Association:

The information provided here will be kept strictly confidential to members of the Ethics Committee and MA staff that work with the committee, but please note that the MA may discuss and share the information you provide to the MA with other museum-sector organisations that are also involved in advising on or assessing your proposal. The MA will keep its advice strictly confidential unless or until the museum's intention to proceed with the proposal for financially motivated disposal enters the public domain. At that point the MA's normal practice is to publish its advice in the interests of transparency and accountability. If a proposal for financially motivated disposal is not in the public domain, or is abandoned, the MA will keep its advice confidential. The MA may in this case seek the museum's permission to publish the advice, or refer to advice we have given in general terms, but without identifying the museum concerned.

Accreditation Assessment Organisations:

AAOs will not volunteer information, but as public bodies they may be subject to Freedom of Information requests. Therefore they are not able to guarantee that all information will be kept confidential.

Please answer the following questions (additional material can also be submitted as evidence to support your answers):

1. Name of museum	
2. Name of organisation owning items being considered for sale (if different)	

3. Your name and contact details:	
4. Please provide a description of the item(s) that are being proposed for sale: (*you might wish to include a photograph along with a full description or an extract from your accession register*)	

5. How will the proposed disposal significantly improve the long-term public benefit derived from the remaining collection and *how will the proposed disposal serve the long-term local and general public interest?*

6. The proposed disposal should not be to generate short-term revenue (for example to meet a budget deficit); please outline how the proceeds from the sale will be used?

7. Please outline how the proposed disposal is a last resort after other sources of
   funding have been thoroughly explored?

8. What extensive prior consultation with sector bodies has been undertaken?

9. How have the views of stakeholders and those who have a vested interest in a
   proposed disposal been sought (for example, donors, researchers, local and source
   communities and others served by the museum)?

10. How do(es) the item(s) under consideration lie outside the museum's established core collection as defined in the collections development policy?
    As part of this please:
    • Explain how the disposal relates to the museum's long-term collections development policy.
    • Give details of the process the museum followed to define its core collection, including details of any collections review.
    • State any external advice that the museum sought to help define the core collection and determine whether the items lie outside the core collection. (Please enclose copies of any external advice.)
    • State when the museum's collections development policy was last revised or reviewed. (Please provide a copy of your current and previous collections development policy.)

11. How will the museum restrict any money raised as a result of the disposal solely and directly for the benefit of the museum's collection? Money raised must be restricted to the long-term sustainability, use, and development of the collection. Please outline any mechanisms that will be put in place to restrict the money for that purpose:

12. In general when disposing of items, the Code of Ethics says "Give priority to transferring items to accredited museums. To maintain public confidence in museums wherever possible do not transfer items out of the public domain." Please explain how you have taken this into account:

Selected Bibliography

American Alliance of Museums. "America's Museums Reflect Slow Economic Recovery in 2012." Arlington, VA: American Alliance of Museums, 2013.

———. "Don't Raid the Cookie Jar—A Few Thoughts About Risk Factors." *Alliance* (blog), March 29, 2018. https://www.aam-us.org/2018/03/29/dont-raid-the-cookie -jar-a-few-thoughts-about-risk-factors/.

———. "Ethics, Guidelines, and Recommendations: Direct Care of Collections." Arlington, VA: American Alliance of Museums, 2019. First published 2016.

———. RE: Aid for Museums Impacted by Coronavirus. Letter to Speaker Pelosi and Leaders McConnell, McCarthy, and Schumer. Arlington, VA: American Alliance of Museums, March 2020.

———. "United States May Lose One-third of All Museums, New Survey Shows." Press Release. Arlington, VA: American Alliance of Museums, July 22, 2020.

Argyris, Chris. *Teaching Smart People to Learn*. Boston: Harvard Business School Press, 2008.

Association of Art Museum Directors. "AAMD Board of Trustees Approves Resolution to Provide Additional Financial Flexibility to Art Museums During Pandemic Crisis." Press Releases & Statements, April 15, 2020. https://aamd.org/for-the -media/press-release/aamd-board-of-trustees-approves-resolution-to-provide -additional.

Bautista, Susana, Elena Brokaw, and Jeannette Kihs. "Museums on the Edge: Stories of Transformation and Failure." Online presentation at the California Association of Museums Lunch & Learn, March 6, 2020. https://www.youtube.com/ watch?v=WhWF59i3rrA&t=3s.

Bruder, Lee. "Nonprofit Dissolution: What to Do When Closing the Doors." *Nonprofit Quarterly*, August 18, 2017. https://nonprofitquarterly.org/nonprofit -dissolution-what-to-do-when-closing-the-doors/.

California Law, Civil Code–CIV, Division 2, Part 3, Title 2, Chapter 3: Products of the Mind [980–989] (987), enacted 1872, amended by Stats. 1994, Ch. 1010, Sec. 30, effective January 1, 1995. California Legislative Information. http://leginfo.legislature.ca.gov/faces/codes_displaySection.xhtml?lawCode=CIV&secionNum=987.

Catlin-Legutko, Cinnamon, and Stacy Klingler, eds. *Small Museum Toolkit*. Lanham, MD: Rowman & Littlefield, 2012.

Carrick-Davies, Stephen. "Closing the Door Gently—Lessons in Closing a Charity." *HuffPost*, September 30, 2016. https://www.huffingtonpost.co.uk/stephen-carrick davies/closing-the-door-gently-l_b_12243878.html.

"Causes of the Recent Financial and Economic Crisis: Testimony Before the Financial Crisis Inquiry Commission." Washington, DC: Statements and Speeches of Ben S. Bernanke, Chairman, Board of Governors of the Federal Reserve System, September 2, 2010.

Commission on Government Forecasting and Accountability. "Illinois State Museum." Accessed September 28, 2020. https://cgfa.ilga.gov/resource.aspx?id=1822.

Dubb, Steve. "Museum Unions Seek More than Improved Pay, Union Organizers Insist." *Nonprofit Quarterly*, March 3, 2020.

Eisenstein, Lena. "What is Government Management and Why is it Important?" *BoardEffect* (blog), November 13, 2019. https://www.boardeffect.com/blog/what-governance-management-important/.

Fobes, Aaron, and Julia Lawless. "Hatch Concludes Review into Tax-Exempt Private Museums, Notes Concerning Findings." Chairman's News, United States Senate Committee on Finance, June 2, 2016. https://www.finance.senate.gov/chairmans-news/hatch-concludes-review-into-tax-exempt-private-museums-notes-concerning-findings.

French, Ferdinand Courtney. "The Concept of Law in Ethics." *Philosophical Review* 2, no. 1 (January 1892): 35–53. Durham, NC: Duke University Press.

Fullerton, Don. "Tax Policy Towards Art Museums." In *The Economics of Art Museums*, edited by Martin Feldstein, 195–236. Chicago: University of Chicago Press, 1991.

Gage, Deborah. "The Venture Capital Secret: 3 Out of 4 Start-Ups Fail." *Wall Street Journal*, September 20, 2012.

Gammon, Martin. *Deaccessioning and Its Discontents: A Critical History*. Cambridge, MA: MIT Press, 2018.

Graham, Stephen, and Nigel Thrift. "Out of Order: Understanding Repair and Maintenance." *Theory, Culture & Society* 24, no. 3 (2007): 1–25.

Hopkins, Bruce R. *The Law of Tax-Exempt Organizations*, 9th edition. Hoboken, NJ: John Wiley & Sons, 2007.

Kelley, Sean. "Mistakes Were Made and Survived." *INSITE Magazine*, Museums Australia Victoria. September/October 2013.

Klees, Emerson. *Entrepreneurs in History—Success vs. Failure*. Unabridged, vol. 2, in *Role Models of Human Values*. Rochester, NY: Cameo Press, 1995.

Manjarrez, Carlos, Celeste Colgan, and Erica Pastore. *Exhibiting Public Value: Museum Public Finance in the United States* (IMLS-2008-RES-02). Washington, DC: Institute of Museum and Library Services, 2008. https://www.imls.gov/sites/default/files/publications/documents/museumpublicfinance_0.pdf.

Marsden, Greg, et al. "Studying Disruptive Events: Innovations in Behaviour, Opportunities for Lower Carbon Transport Policy?" *Transport Policy* 94 (2020): 89–101.

Masaoka, Jan. "Closing Down the Right Way." *Blue Avocado*, October 1, 2008. Nonprofits Insurance Alliance. https://blueavocado.org/finance/closing-down-the-right-way/.

Maxwell, John C. *Failing Forward: Turning Mistakes Into Stepping Stones for Success*. Nashville, TN: Thomas Nelson, 2000.

McGrath, Rita Gunther. "Failing by Design." *Harvard Business Review*, April 2011. Accessed August 1, 2020. https://hbr.org/2011/04/failing-by-design.

Meier, Allison C. "Resting in Pieces: The Scattered Fate of Closed Museums," *Hyperallergic*, September 20, 2013. https://hyperallergic.com/84447/resting-in-pieces-the-scattered-fate-of-closed-museums/.

Merritt, Elizabeth. "Failing Toward Success: The Ascendance of Agile Design." *Museum*, March/April 2017. Arlington, VA: American Alliance of Museums.

———. "Helping Museums Navigate Through the COVID-19 Fog." Interview by Wallace Blog editorial team, Wallace Foundation, June 4, 2020. https://www.wallacefoundation.org/news-and-media/blog/pages/helping-museums-navigate-through-the-covid-19-fog.aspx.

———. "Law and Ethics: An Ounce of Prevention." *Museum*, July/August 2009. Arlington, VA: American Alliance of Museums.

———. "Three New Scenarios for Financial Survival in 2020." Center for the Future of Museums Blog, April 13, 2020. Arlington, VA: American Alliance of Museums.

Miller, Francine Koslow. *Cashing In on Culture: Betraying the Trust at the Rose Art Museum*. Tucson, AZ: Hol Art, 2012.

Moe, Richard. "Are There Too Many House Museums?" *Forum Journal* 27, no. 1 (Fall 2012): 55–61. https://www.muse.jhu.edu/article/494513.

———. "Q&A with Richard Moe." By Brian Lamb. *Q&A*. C-Span, January 18, 2006. https://www.c-span.org/video/?190799-1/qa-richard-moe.

Morris, Martha. "Are Museums Recession-Proof?" *Museum*, January/February 2010. Arlington, VA: American Alliance of Museums.

Morse, Eric. "Why Employees at the Philadelphia Museum of Art are Unionizing." *Art Museum Teaching*, July 17, 2020.

Nazarov, Amy Rogers. "Ethical Considerations for Museum Closures," American Alliance of Museums, Mission & Institutional Planning, July 1, 2009. https://www.aam-us.org/2009/07/01/ethical-considerations-for-museum-closures/.

Nolan, Tina R. "From the Interim Editor in Chief: History Repeats Itself: American Museums in a Time of Recession. Will We Ever Learn?" *Journal of Museum Education* 35, no. 1 (2010): 117–20. Accessed December 6, 2020. http://www.jstor.org/stable/25701648.

Ogilvy, Jay. "Scenario Planning and Strategic Forecasting." *Forbes*, January 8, 2015. https://www.forbes.com/sites/stratfor/2015/01/08/scenario-planning-and-strategic-forecasting/#798869c3411a.

Peek, Sean. "How to Know if You Really Classify as a Small Business." *Business News Daily*, August 4, 2020.

Phelan, Marilyn E. *Museum Law: A Guide for Officers, Directors, and Counsel.* 4th ed. Lanham, MD: Rowman & Littlefield, 2014.

Rogers Nazarov, Amy. "Ethical Considerations for Museum Closures." *Museum*, July/August 2009. Arlington, VA: American Alliance of Museums.

Scott, Carol. "Museums, the Public, and Public Value." *Journal of Museum Education* 35, no. 1 (2010): 33–42. http://www.jstor.org/stable/25701639.

"Shutdown Prevention and Economic Impact Issue Brief," American Alliance of Museums, 2019. https://www.aam-us.org/programs/advocacy/policy-issues/.

Siegal, Nina. "Many Museums Won't Survive the Virus. How Do You Close One Down?" *New York Times*, April 29, 2020. https://www.nytimes.com/2020/04/29/arts/design/how-do-you-close-a-museum.html.

Singer, Natalie. "Bellevue Arts [sic] Museum Set to Reopen in Late Spring. *Seattle Times*, April 2, 2005.

Small Business Administration (SBA), Office of Advocacy. "Do Economic or Industry Factors Affect Business Survival?" Small Business Facts, June 2012. https://www.sba.gov/sites/default/files/Business-Survival.pdf.

Smith, Gary N. "If It Is Time To Close It: Considerations for Dissolving An Organization." Dallas, TX: Summerlee Foundation, 2018.

Stevens, Susan Kenny. *Nonprofit Lifecycles; Stage-Based Wisdom for Nonprofit Capacity.* Long Lake, MN: Stagewise Enterprises, 2001.

Stiglitz, Joseph. "Inequality, Wealth, and Capital." *Queries* 7 (Summer 2015): 56–59.

Turino, Kenneth C. "America Doesn't Need Another House Museum." *History News* 64, no. 2 (Spring 2009).

UK Public General Acts. "Equality Act 2010." Accessed September 10, 2020. https://www.legislation.gov.uk/ukpga/2010/15/contents.

Wetenhall, John. "'Til Death Do Us Part . . .': Prenuptials for a Museum Merger." Unpublished paper, September 2020.

Woronkowicz, Joanna, et al. *Set in Stone: Building America's New Generation of Arts Facilities, 1994–2008* (Chicago: University of Chicago, Cultural Policy Center, 2012).

RESOURCES

American Alliance of Museums, https://www.aam-us.org/
- *Alliance* Blog
- Center for the Future of Museums Blog
- Closing Permanently (AAM membership required)

- Code of Ethics, https://www.aam-us.org/programs/ethics-standards-and-professional-practices/code-of-ethics-for-museums/
- "Ethics, Standards and Professional Practices: Questions and Answers about Selling Objects from the Collection"
- *Museum* magazine
- Resource Library (AAM membership required)
- "TrendsWatch 2018: The Scenario Edition. A Tool for Museum Planning"

American Association for State and Local History, https://aaslh.org/
- AASLH Committee on Professional Standards and Ethics. "When a History Museum Closes." Ethics Position Paper #2. *History News* (June 2006)
- AASLH Council. "Valuing History Collections." Blog (May 2020)
- AASLH Historic House Affinity Group Committee. "How Sustainable Is Your Historic House Museum?" Technical Leaflet #244. *History News* (Autumn 2008)
- AASLH Standing Committee on Standards and Ethics. "Repurposing of a Historic House/Site." Ethics Position Paper #3. *History News* (Spring 2009)
- AASLH Statement of Standards and Ethics (Revised 2018)
- Beard, Rick. "When a History Museum Closes." Ethics Position Paper #2. *History News* (Summer 2007)

American Planning Association, https://www.planning.org/knowledgebase/scenario planning/
- Scenario Planning

American Society of Quality, https://asq.org/quality-resources/iso-26000
- Learn About Quality: ISO 26000

Americans for the Arts, https://www.americansforthearts.org/
- ARTSblog
- ArtsU

Council on Foundations, https://www.cof.org/foundation-type/community-foundations-taxonomy
- Community Foundations

Fail Forward, https://failforward.org/resources#materials
- Resources: Ideas and Tools to Help Your Organization Take Risks, Learn, Adapt and Fail Intelligently

Failed Museums, http://miriamposner.com/omeka/exhibits/show/fail/intro
- Miriam Posner, PhD (assistant professor of information studies and digital humanities at the University of California, Los Angeles)

The Federal Emergency Management Agency (FEMA), https://www.ready.gov/
- Ready Business

Foundation for Advancement in Conservation, https://www.culturalheritage.org/about-us/foundation
- Connecting to Collections Care
- Klein, Janice. "Making a Good End: How to Close a Museum." Handout. EightSixSix Consulting. http://www.connectingtocollections.org/wp-content/uploads/2018/10/Handout_Making-a-Good-End.pdf

- ———. "Making a Good End: How to Close a Museum." Webinar recorded on November 13, 2018. https://www.connectingtocollections.org/close-a-museum/

Internal Revenue Service

"'Charitable' Purposes," https://www.irs.gov/charities-non-profits/charitable-purposes
- "Exemption Requirements—501(c)(3) Organizations," https://www.irs.gov/charities-non-profits/charitable-organizations/exemption-requirements-501c3-organizations
- "How Long Should I Keep Records?," https://www.irs.gov/businesses/small-businesses-self-employed/how-long-should-i-keep-records
- "Life Cycle of a Private Foundation," https://www.irs.gov/pub/irs-tege/Life_Cycle_Private_Foundation_graphical.pdf
- "Life Cycle of a Public Charity," https://www.irs.gov/charities-non-profits/charitable-organizations/life-cycle-of-a-public-charity
- "Maintaining 501(c)(3) Tax Exempt Status," https://www.stayexempt.irs.gov/home/existing-organizations/maintaining-501c3-tax-exempt-status
- "Suggested Language for Corporations and Associations," https://www.irs.gov/charities-non-profits/suggested-language-for-corporations-and-associations
- Tax Exempt and Government Entities Division. "Facts about Terminating or Merging Your Exempt Organization." Publication 4779 (May 2009). www.irs.gov/pub/irs-pdf/p4779.pdf
- "Tax Exempt Status for Your Organization (per Publication 557)," https://www.irs.gov/pub/irs-pdf/p557.pdf
- "Termination of an Exempt Organization," https://www.irs.gov/charities-non-profits/termination-of-an-exempt-organization

Museums Association, United Kingdom, https://www.museumsassociation.org
- Compliance Report for Financially Motivated Disposal of Items from a Museum Collection
- "Disposal Toolkit: Guidelines for Museums." Collections Trust (2014)
- "Museums Facing Closure: Legal and Ethical Issues." Collections Trust (2017)
- Ulph, Janet. "The Legal and Ethical Status of Museum Collections: Curatorially Motivated Disposals." University of Leicester, September 2016

National Council of Nonprofits, https://www.councilofnonprofits.org
- Board Roles and Responsibilities: Tools & Resources
- Dissolving a Nonprofit Corporation

National Trust for Historic Preservation, https://realestate.savingplaces.org/
- Historic Properties for Sale
- *Preservation* magazine

The Netherlands Museums Association (Museumvereniging), https://www.museumvereniging.nl/media/lamo_2016_guidelines_for_the_deaccessioning_of_museum_objects_1.pdf
- "Guideline for Deaccessioning Museum Objects" (Leidraad voor het Afstoten van Museale Objecten/LAMO) (2016)

NOLO, https://www.nolo.com/

- "50-State Guide to Dissolving a 501(c)(3) Corporation," https://www.nolo.com/legal-encyclopedia/50-state-guide-dissolving-501c3-nonprofit-corporation

Nonprofit Lifecycles Institute, https://nonprofitlifecycles.com/institute/
- Susan Kenny Stevens, PhD (nonprofit consultant)

Nonprofit Quarterly magazine, https://nonprofitquarterly.org/

ProPublica, https://projects.propublica.org/nonprofits/ctypes
- Nonprofit Explorer

Public Counsel, http://www.publiccounsel.org
- "Guide for Reinstatement of Good Standing with Corporate and Tax Regulatory Agencies for California Nonprofit Public Benefit Corporations" (Revised January 2017)
- "Guide for the Dissolution of California Nonprofit Public Benefit Corporations," Community Development Project (Revised January 2017)

Stanford D. School, https://dschool.stanford.edu/resources/getting-started-with-design-thinking
- "Get Started with Design Thinking." Hasso Plattner Institute of Design at Stanford University

StateAG.org, https://www.stateag.org/
- James E. Tierney (former Maine Attorney General, former Director of the National State Attorneys General Program at Columbia Law School)

UNESCO (United Nations Educational, Scientific and Cultural Organization), https://en.unesco.org/
- ResiliArt

US Chamber of Commerce—CO, https://www.uschamber.com/co
- Peek, Sean. "Ready to Move On? How to Create an Exit Plan for Your Business" (March 7, 2019).

US Small Business Administration, https://www.sba.gov/
- "Business Guide. Manage Your Business. Close or Sell Your Business"
- "SBA Disaster Field Offices"
- "SBA Learning Platform. Learning Center"

INFORMATION ON SELECTED STATES

California

Attorney General's Office, "General Guide for Dissolving a California Nonprofit Corporation," https://oag.ca.gov/sites/all/files/agweb/pdfs/charities/publications/dissolving.pdf.

Franchise Tax Board, "Guide to Dissolve, Surrender, or Cancel a California Business Entity," https://www.ftb.ca.gov/forms/misc/1038.html.

Secretary of State, Business Programs Division, "California Nonprofit Corporation Dissolution Requirements—What Form to File," http://bpd.cdn.sos.ca.gov/corp/pdf/dissolutions/corp_npdiss.pdf.

Delaware

Division of Corporations, "Certificate of Dissolution: Short Form," https://corpfiles
.delaware.gov/Dissolution%20-%20275%20Short%20Form%20-%20web.pdf.

District of Columbia

Office of the Attorney General for the District of Columbia, "Charities and
Other Nonprofit Organizations," https://oag.dc.gov/charities-and-other-nonprofit
-organizations.

Florida

Department of State, Division of Corporations. "E-File Articles of Dissolution,"
https://dos.myflorida.com/sunbiz/manage-business/dissolve-withdraw-business/
efile-corporation-dissolution/.

Georgia

Probono Partnership/Atlanta, "Dissolving a Georgia Nonprofit Corporation," https://
www.pbpatl.org/wp-content/uploads/2015/01/DISSOLVING-A-GEORGIA
-NONPROFIT-ORGANIZATION.pdf.

Illinois

Chicago Lawyers' Committee for Civil Rights, Community Law Project, "A
Guide for Nonprofit Organizations: Dissolution of Illinois Not For Profit
Corporations," 2nd edition (May 2013), https://static1.squarespace.com/static/
5871061e6b8f5b2a8ede8ff5/t/5b0712df2b6a283129114bd7/1527190243235/
Dissolution+Book+2013+FINAL.pdf.

Massachusetts

Mass.gov, "Guide: Dissolving a Charity," https://www.mass.gov/guides/dissolving
-a-charity.

Michigan

Department of Attorney General, "Dissolution Questionnaire," https://www
.michigan.gov/documents/f021-mast_dis_quest_40909_7.pdf.
Michigan Department of Licensing and Regulatory Affairs, Corporations, Securities
& Commercial Licensing Bureau, "Dissolution: Profit Corporations and Limited

Liability Companies," https://www.michigan.gov/documents/lara/8007_528147_7
.pdf.

Minnesota

Minnesota State Bar Association, Nonprofit Corporations Committee of the Business
Law Section, "Guide for the Voluntary Dissolution of Minnesota Nonprofit Corpo-
rations," http://legalcorps.org/wp-content/uploads/2012/03/LegalCorps-Nonprofit
-Dissolution-Guidelines.pdf.

New Mexico

New Mexico Association of Grantmakers, Center for Nonprofit Excellence, "How to
Close a Nonprofit in New Mexico," https://www.centerfornonprofitexcellence.org/
ending-nonprofit.
New Mexico Secretary of State, Business Services, "Domestic NM Nonprofit Corporation," https://www.sos.state.nm.us/business-services/business-maintenance/
domestic-nm-nonprofit-corporation/.

New York

New York State Office of the Attorney General, Charities, "Voluntary Dissolution of
New York State Not-For-Profit Corporations with Assets," https://www.charities
nys.com/pdfs/dissolution_with_assets.pdf, and "FAQs–Simplified Dissolutions,"
https://www.charitiesnys.com/faqs_dissolutions_new.html.

North Carolina

North Carolina Bar Association and the N.C. Center for Nonprofits, "Guidebook
for Boards of Directors of North Carolina Nonprofit Corporations," 2nd edition,
https://clearviewfiduciary.com/assets/pdfs/Guidebook-2ed.pdf.

Ohio

Ohio Attorney General, Charitable Ohio, "Nonprofit Transactions, Probate & Court
Proceedings," https://charitable.ohioago.gov/Charitable-Transactions.
Ohio Laws and Rules, Ohio Administrative Code, Title XVII, Corporations-Partner
ships, Chapter 1702: Nonprofit Corporation Law, "1702.47 Voluntary dissolution,"
http://codes.ohio.gov/orc/1702.47.

Oregon

Nonprofit Association of Oregon, "How Do I Dissolve My Nonprofit Corporation?,"
https://nonprofitoregon.org/helpline_resources/tools_information/faqs/dissolution.

Rhode Island

Rhode Island Department of State, Business Services, Non Profit, "Close Your Non-Profit in Rhode Island," https://www.sos.ri.gov/divisions/business-services/non -profit/close-your-non-profit-corporation.

Washington State

King County Bar Association, "Washington Nonprofit Handbook," https://communities -rise.org/resources/washington-nonprofit-handbook/.

Index

About the Author

Susana Smith Bautista is a museophile and an art historian. Her professional, academic, and personal experiences are very diverse and unconventional, but the two threads that run through them are museums and art. Susana received a PhD in communication from the University of Southern California, with the understanding that museums are fundamentally based on various systems and theories of communication. After researching digital communication technologies and how they affect museums, she published her dissertation as *Museums in the Digital Age: Changing Meanings of Place, Community, and Culture* (2013). Susana completed her master's degree in art history/museum studies with honors (Phi Kappa Phi) also at USC. Her focus as an art historian is Chicano/a, Latino/a, and Latin American art, which she also pursued as an art critic and curator while living in New York, Greece, and Los Angeles. She has held various leadership positions, including executive director of the Mexican Cultural Institute of Los Angeles, interim deputy director and director of public engagement at the USC Pacific Asia Museum, executive director of the Pasadena Museum of California Art, editorial director of LatinArt.com, senior curator-at-large for LA Plaza de Cultura y Artes, and Arts and Culture Commissioner for the City of Pasadena. Susana has taught at USC Annenberg School for Communication and at Claremont Graduate University's Arts Management program. She has also been invited to lecture around the world and has published numerous articles and book chapters on museums. She serves on the Board of Trustees for the American Alliance of Museums, where she is a peer reviewer in the Museum Assessment Program and member of the inaugural Board Diversity Committee. Susana is presently the director and chief curator of the AltaMed Art Collection. Find out more about Susana at www.susanasmithbautista.com.

Lightning Source UK Ltd.
Milton Keynes UK
UKHW051339270422
402083UK00021B/49